Prentice Mulford

The God in You
(Unabridged)

e-artnow 2018

Reading suggestions (available from e-artnow as Print & eBook)

Prentice Mulford
Your Forces and How to Use Them (Six Volumes - Complete Edition)

Prentice Mulford
Thoughts Are Things & The God In You - Connect With The Force Within Yourself

William Walker Atkinson
PERSONAL POWER (All 12 Volumes)

William Walker Atkinson
MASTER MIND - The Key To Mental Power Development And Efficiency

Prentice Mulford
The Prentice Mulford Premium Collection: "New Thought" Studies, Novels & Memoirs

William Walker Atkinson
THE ARCANE TEACHINGS - Complete Collection: The Arcane Formulas - Mental Alchemy, The Arcane Teachings & Vril - The Vital Magnetism

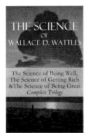

Wallace D. Wattles
The Science of Wallace D. Wattles: The Science of Being Well, The Science of Getting Rich & The Science of Being Great - Complete Trilogy

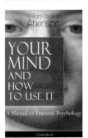

William Walker Atkinson
Your Mind and How to Use It: A Manual of Practical Psychology (Unabridged)

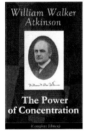

William Walker Atkinson
The Power of Concentration (Complete Edition): Life lessons and concentration exercises: Learn how to develop and improve the invaluable power of concentration

William Walker Atkinson
THOUGHT VIBRATION - The Law of Attraction in the Thought World (Unabridged)

Prentice Mulford

The God in You
(Unabridged)

From one of the New Thought pioneers, author of Thoughts are Things, Your Forces and How to Use Them, Gift of Spirit, Swamp Angel, Life By Land and Sea and The Gift of Understanding

e-artnow, 2018
Contact: info@e-artnow.org

ISBN 978-80-268-9158-1

Contents

INTRODUCTION

THERE is a gospel older than Christianity, older than Buddhism, older than Brahmanism, older than the classic religions of Greece and Rome, older than the worship of idols and the worship of ancestors. This gospel has been preached under varying forms and names, and with stress laid upon different aspects of its truth and its applicability to differing conditions of civilisation and to the different characters of the peoples to whom the message has been addressed. It is probably as old as the earliest traditions of civilised man, and the preaching of it becomes a periodical necessity through the very evolution and growth of civilisation itself. It acts as an alternative medicine, a corrective of the tendency inherent in civilisation to drift insensibly into channels of artificiality, to substitute the letter for the spirit, the creed for the life, the formula for the thing signified, habit for deliberate conscious action, the cant catchword for the life-giving principle, the spurious imitation for the genuine product. The Gospel to which I allude Is the Gospel of the Return to Nature.

In every generation of the world's history since man was civilised, the realisation of this state has been the dream of a few idealists who saw it existing in the far distant past of the world's history in an allegorical form as the fabled Golden Age sung of by the poets. If it is older than all the religions, it yet takes its place as an essential element of all of them in the first stages of their existence. Jesus Christ struck the keynote in his preaching when he bade his disciples "suffer the little children to come unto me, for of such is the Kingdom of Heaven," and again when he said, "Except ye be born again as a little child ye cannot enter into the Kingdom of Heaven." And the refrain of very many of his injunctions to his disciples was the adoption of what we should now call the Simple Life so much talked about but so little lived in these days of the twentieth century. Buddha gave expression to the same thought and practised it in his renunciation of his princely life and his adoption of the life of the wondering preacher, of the begging friar. The same truth was inculcated in China by Lao-tsze and again to a later age, in France, by Jean Jacques Rousseau in his *Social Contract and his Discourse on the Origin of Inequality among Men.*"

Man is born free, and yet everywhere he is in chains." Such were the opening words of this inspiring message to the Peoples of the Earth. Man is born natural and civilisation makes him artificial. He is born in touch with Nature and life under the open sky and in the green fields. Civilisation draws him to courts and towns. Mankind is born to liberty and equality: civilisation makes him either a tyrant on the one hand or a slave on the other. The thought underlying this gospel, whether preached by Christ or by Rousseau, or today by Edward Carpenter in his *Civilisation, its Cause and Cure*, contrasted as the characters of the preachers will appear, is essentially the same.

Why were the Scribes and Pharisees hypocrites? Why, except because they had turned from the spirit to the letter, from Nature to artificiality? What was the crime of the French Monarchy but that it fostered and perpetuated unnatural conditions and artificial restrictions which froze the life-blood of the French people? What were the faults which Prentice Mulford saw in American civilisation, if they were not the faults which arise directly from the too rapid growth of the luxuries and so-called advantages which civilisation and commercial development bring in their train, and from the neglect of those forces which are inherent in Nature itself and without which the life-blood of a nation of necessity becomes contaminated and impoverished?

"You are fortunate (writes Prentice Mulford) if you love trees, and especially the wild ones growing where the great Creative Force placed them and independent of man's care. For all things that we call wild or natural are nearer the Infinite Mind than those which have been enslaved, artificialised and hampered by man. Being nearer the Infinite, they have in them the more perfect infinite force and thought. That is why, when you are in the midst of what is wild and natural, where every trace of man's works is left behind, you feel an indescribable exhilaration and freedom that you do not realise elsewhere."

This sentence seems to me to strike a note of the greatest importance in connection with all these "Return to Nature" movements in whatever period of the world's history they may have occurred. It is especially noteworthy how each movement of the kind has been followed by a great uprising of the life forces of the nation or nations to whom it was preached. It acts on the generation which listens to its preaching like the winds of spring on the sap of winter trees. It is the great revivals consequent on such preaching that let loose the pent-up energies of the human race and in doing so make the great epochs of history. Christianity was the result of one such great movement. The French Revolution was the result of such another.

The gospel of Rousseau was preached not to the French nation only. It was preached in France, it is true, but it was preached to mankind at large, and the fact that it was listened to by many nations outside France is more than half the explanation of the triumphs of Napoleon, the heir of the new French Democracy. In the early days of his triumph Napoleon came to the peoples of the other countries of Europe as much in the guise of a deliverer as of a conqueror. The soldiers that fought in the armies against him had heard the message of freedom and equality and were in no mood to contend with its conquering arm. The gospel according to Jean Jacques Rousseau was this life-giving force. Like a tonic breath from the sea, like a draught of champagne, it was at the same time invigorating and intoxicating to its hearers. Prentice Mulford was right, the Gospel of Nature, wherever preached, "has ever made man feel an indescribable exhilaration and freedom."

Where Mulford differed from Rousseau was in seeing more clearly, more spiritually, what the Return to Nature really signified. That it signified the getting in touch once more i: with "the Infinite Force and Mind as expressed by all natural things." This Spirit of Nature, "this Force of the Infinite Mind," was given out, he maintained, by every wild tree, bird, or animal. It was a literal element and force, going to man from tree and from living creature. If you loved Nature, if you loved the trees, you would find them, declared Mulford, responsive to such love.

"You are fortunate (he says) when you grow to a live, tender, earnest love for the wild trees, animals, and birds, and recognise them all as coming from and built of the same mind and spirit as your own, and able also to give you something very valuable in return for the love which you give them. The wild tree is not irresponsive or regardless of a love like that. Such love is not a myth or mere sentiment. It is a literal element and force going from you to the tree. It is felt by the spirit of the tree. You represent a part and belonging of the Infinite Mind. The tree represents another part and belonging of the Infinite Mind. It has its share of life, thought, and intelligence. You have a far greater share, which is to be greater still--and then still greater."

And again:–

"As the Great Spirit has made all things, is not that All-pervading mind and wisdom in all things? If then we love the trees, the rocks and all things, as the Infinite made them, shall they not in response to our love give us each of their peculiar thought and wisdom? Shall we not draw nearer to God through a love for these expressions of God in the rocks and trees, birds and animals?"

Poets have told us the same story. Sir Walter Scott did so, for instance, in his beautiful lines in "The Lay of the Last Minstrel":-

"Call it not vain. They do not err.Who say that, when the poet dies,Mute Nature mourns her worshipperAnd celebrates his obsequies;That say mute crag and cavern loneFor the departed hard make moan,And rivers teach their rushing waveTo murmur dirges o'er his grave."

Wordsworth, too, understood the communion with Nature, as is shown by many of his verses, and most of all by his lines on the vision of the daffodils. The sight of the daffodils dancing by the lake was to him like the midnight dance of fairies or elves on the greensward, instinct with conscious vitality, and the impulse of contagious motion. This picture of the 'daffodils' delight in their own life and beauty recalled itself automatically to the poet's mind, and bade him join them in their fairy revels. No poet could have put the mood of communion with Nature in lines of greater felicity. They are, indeed, well known, but to the lover of Nature they will bear quoting again and again. The poet exclaims:-

" I gazed and gazed, but little thoughtWhat joy the show to me had brought.For oft, when on my couch I lieIn vacant or in pensive mood.They flash upon that inward eyeWhich is the bliss of solitude;And then my heart with pleasure fills,And dances with the daffodils."

Other poets have voiced the same sense of communion with Nature in varying forms and degrees of intensity. A lesser known one of the present day has claimed poetry as Nature's mouthpiece, and condemned its neglect as a refusal to be brought into touch with Nature's many voices by the most articulate means at its disposal. Take the following verses as an example :-

"If thou disdain the sacred Muse,Beware lest Nature, past recall,Indignant at that crime, refuseThee entrance to her audience hall.Beware lest sea and sky and allThat bears reflection of her faceBe blotted with a hueless pallOf unillumined commonplace.Ah! desolate hour when that shall be,When dew and sunlight, rain and windShall seem but trivial things to thee,Unloved, unheeded, undivined!Nay, rather let that morning findThy molten soul exhaled and gone,Than in a living death resignedSo darkly still to labour on."

We see that poets galore have voiced this sentiment and have even expressed it like Sir Waiter Scott in the form of a belief in the conscious Life of Nature. Poets live in a world of fancy and imagination. We do not take their statements too literally. It is different when we come to a man who writes essays, which he would have us take as a guide in life, who, in his wildest flights, expects to be taken as intending to convey the full force of what he says, in however spiritual a sense.

You cannot say of the lines of Scott what the great Earl of Chatham said in quite a differ-ent connection, that " though poetry they are no fiction."* You feel that Scott was by way of expressing a poetic mood, the literal truth of which he would never dream of substantiating over the dinner table, Prentice Mulford, on the other hand, preached this doctrine as an actual truth to be accepted and acted upon, to be made a basis upon which to erect a practical manual on the subject of how to live most intensely, of how, in short, to be most alive while living. Prentice Mulford, in preaching his gospel, echoed in other words the message proclaimed by the Founder of Christianity: "I have come that ye might have life, and that ye might have it more abundantly."

To Mulford every man is an unconsciouspsychometrist. The infection of good or evil is all-pervasive.

"Everything (he tells us) from a stone to a human being sends out to you as you look upon it a certain amount of force affecting you beneficially or injuriously according to the quality of life or animation which it possesses. Take any article of furniture, a chair or a bedstead, for instance. It contains not only the thought of those who first planned and moulded it on its construction, but it is also permeated with the thought and varying moods of all who have sat on it or slept in it. So also are the walls and every article of furniture in any room permeated with the thought of those who have dwelt in it, and if it has been long lived in by people whose lives were narrow, whose occupation varied little from year to year, whose moods were dismal and cheerless, the walls and furniture will be saturated with this gloomy and sickly order of thought.

"If you are very sensitive, and stay in such a room but for a single day, you will feel in some way the depressing effect of such thought, unless you keep very positive to it, and to keep sufficiently positive for twenty-four hours at a time to resist it would be extremely difficult. If you are in any degree weak or ailing you are then most negative or open to the nearest thought- element about you, and will be affected by it, in addition to the wearying mental effect (first mentioned) of any object kept constantly before the eyes.

"It is injurious, then, to be sick, or even wearied, in a room where other people have been sick, or where they have died, because in thought-element all the misery and depression, not only of the sick and dying but of such as gathered there and sympathised with the patient, will be still left in the room, and this is a powerful unseen agent for acting injuriously on the living."

The above quotation is from an essay on " Spells, or the Law of Change"; but our author de-velops the same idea to a fuller extent in another essay, that on "Positive and Negative Thought," in which he enlarges on the importance of being positive and not negative when surrounded by those who are emitting poisonous thought atmosphere, such as envy, jealousy, cynicism, or despondency. This, he tells us, is as real as an noxious gas and infinitely more dangerous. If you are then in a negative or receptive state you are to all intents and purposes a sponge, absorbing evil influences, the full harm of which may not be realised till days afterwards.

You must know, then, when to be in a positive and when in a negative frame of mind. As a rule you must be positive when you have dealings with the world and negative when you retire within yourself. These conditions inevitably alternate one with another, and the exercise of much positive force will bring about a natural reaction after a certain time. Why, asks Prentice Mulford, did the Christ so often withdraw from the multitude? It was, he avers, because after exercising in some way the immense power ofconcentrated thought, either by healing or talking, or by giving some proofs of his command over the physical elements, at which times he was positive and expending his forces, he, feeling the negative state coming upon him, left the crowd so that he should not absorb their lower thought.

Prentice Mulford lays great stress on the reality, indeed, substantiality of thought."As aman thinketh, so is he." "Your spirit," says Mulford, " is a bundle of thought." What you think most of, that is your spirit. " Thought," he says again, " is a substance as much as air, or any other unseen element of which chemistry makes us aware. Strong thought is the same as strong will. Every thought, spoken or unspoken, is a thing as real, though invisible, as water or metal. When you think you work. Every thought represents an outlay of force. If a man thinks murder he actually puts out an element of murder in the air. He sends from him a plan of murder as real as if drawn on paper. If the thought is absorbed by others, it inclines them towards violence, if not murder. If a person is ever thinking of sickness he sends from him the element of sickness. If he thinks of health, strength, and cheerfulness, he sends from him constructions of thought helping others towards health and strength, as well as himself."

In thought every man should look forward and cast the past behind him. " Nature buries its dead as quickly as possible, and gets them out of sight. It is better, however, to say that Nature changes what it has no further use for into other forms of life. The tree produces the new leaf with each return of spring. It will have nothingto do with its dead ones. It treasures up no withered rose leaves to bring back sad remembrance." . . . " Nothing in Nature is at a standstill. A gigantic incomprehensible Wisdom moves all things forward towards greater and higher powers and possibilities. You are included in and are part of this force."

If then, argues Mulford, you do not move forward with the rest of Nature, you will inevitably sink, and rightly sink, into decrepitude and decay. Why are outworn creeds outworn? Simply because they have not changed with the changing thought of man, they have not evolved with the evolution of the race. They have remained behind on a lower plane while man has moved forward to a higher. If you cling to them you cling to what will draw you back and draw you downward. It is the same in business. The business methods of one generation must be changed and modified in order to adapt the business to the conditions and demands of the uprising generation. The "good old times" may have been good in their way, though their goodness is generally exaggerated; but to attempt to revive their ways of thought for the use of later generations is like putting new wine into old bottles.

Prentice Mulford had absorbed among his other ideas the eastern doctrine of metempsychosis. The race had evolved, he held, from the lowest forms. It could, therefore, evolve indefinitely higher. Man, as at present constituted, was not its ultimate aim. The possibilities of human evolution were infinite.

"It is a grand mistake (he writes), that of supposing that any man or woman is the result of that

one short life which we live here. We have all lived possibly in various forms as animal, bird, snake, insect, plant. Our starting-point of matter in existence has been dragged on the sea's bottom, embedded in icebergs, and vomited out of volcanoes amid fire, smoke and ashes. It has been tossed about on the ocean and has lain maybe for centuries and centuries embedded in the heart of some Pleiocene mountain. We have crept up and up, now in one form, now in another, always gaining something more in intelligence, something more of force, by each change, until at last here we are, nor have we got far along yet."

If man's power of developing is indefinite it follows, thinks Mulford, that his power of prolonging life is also limitless; i.e. not merely prolonging life under other conditions outside the physical body, but even of prolonging life within the physical body itself. Hence his essay dealing with Immortality in the Flesh--an essay which more than any other has led to Mulford being dubbed a crank and a mad dreamer. " We believe," he writes, "that immortality in the flesh is a possibility, or in other words, that a physical body can be retained so long as the spirit desires its use, and that this body instead of decreasing in strength and vigour as the years go on, will increase and its youth will be perpetual."

There is a Law (says Mulford) of Silent Demand, and silent continuous demand made with concentration of will and thought can obtain whatever it asks for--whatever it claims as its own, in view of the fact that each human being is part of the Infinite Life and has inalienable relationship to the Supreme Power. "There will be built," our author predicts, "in time, an edifice partaking of the nature of a church where allpersons of whatever condition, age, nationality, or creed may come to lay their needs before the great Supreme Power and demand of that Power help to supply those needs. It should be a church without sect or creed. It should be open every day during the week and every evening until a reasonable hour. It should be a place of silence for the purpose of silent demand or prayer. It should be a place of earnest demand for permanent good, yet not a place of gloom. A church should be held as a sanctuary for the concentration of the strongest thought power. The strongest thought power is where the motive is the highest. You can get such power by unceasing silent demand of the Supreme Power of which you are a part."

This power of silent demand can be utilised, then, for all purposes. It can be utilised, for instance, to keep the body in health, to make good the wearing away of the tissues, to prevent the ageing and final perishing of the physical body. "The body is continually changing its elements in accordance with the condition of the mind. If it is in certain mental conditions, it is conveying to itself elements of decay, weakness, and physical death. If in another mental condition, it is adding to itself elements of strength and life. That which the spirit takes on in either case is thought or belief. Thoughts and beliefs materialise themselves in flesh and blood. Belief in inevitable decay and death brings from the spirit to the body the elements of decay and death. Belief in the possibility of a constant inflowing to the spirit of life brings life."

These ideas, as I have already suggested, seemfairly far-fetched. But it is a curious fact that science does not appear to reject them quite as decisively as one would have expected. Messrs. Carrington & Meader, in their book on *Death, its Causes and Phenomena*, which bears very directly on this interesting question, quote the observation of a physician, Dr. William A. Hammond: "There is no physiological reason why man should die," and also Dr. Monroe in his statement that the "human body as a machine is perfect. It is apparently intended to go on forever." And again, they cite the observation of Dr. Thomas J. Allen, who states that "the body is self-renewing and should not therefore wear out by constant disintegration."

The point is not so much perhaps that *natural death*, as we call it, is unnatural, as that the reason why mankind die after a certain age has never been satisfactorily explained from a medical point of view, and the medical evidence points to the fact not so much that man might conceivably be immortal as that the process of decay might be indefinitely retarded. That, in short, man might live to a far greater age than he does at present.

There is a great deal in Prentice Mulford which seems commonplace enough today. Men of the twentieth century are familiar with his doctrines and his teachings. They have been put forward with a great air of originality by many of his followers, and they have been repeated in various forms and with varying degrees of exaggeration. I doubt, however, if they have ever been put forward so freshly and so forcibly as they were by the pioneer of what we now call the New Thought Movement--Prentice Mulford. There is in no other leader of this New Thought Movement such a sense of the communion with Nature, so fresh and full a recognition of the possibility of utilising Nature's forces for the benefit of body and spirit. For, as I have already explained, Prentice Mulford was, not only the first and greatest of the New Thought teachers, but also par excellence an apostle of the Return to Nature.RALPH SHIRLEY.

Chapter 1
POSITIVE AND NEGATIVE THOUGHT

YOUR mind or spirit is continually giving out its force or thought, or receiving some quality of such force, as an electric battery may be sending out its energy and may be afterwards replenished. When you use your force in talking, or writing, or physical effort of any sort, you are positive. When not so using it, you are negative. When negative, or receptive, you are receiving force or element of some kind or quality, which may do you temporary harm or permanent good.

All evil of any kind is but temporary. Your spirit's course through all successive lives is toward the condition of ever-increasing and illimitable happiness.

There are poisonous atmospheres of thought as real as the poisonous fumes of arsenic or other metallic vapours. You may, if negative, in a single hour, by sitting in a room with persons whose minds are full of envy, jealousy, cynicism or despondency, absorb from them a literally poisonous element of thought, full of disease. It is as real as any noxious gas, vapour or miasma. It is infinitely more dangerous, so subtle is its working, for the full injury may not be realised till days afterwards, and is then attributed to some other cause.

It is of the greatest importance where you are, or by what element of thought, emanating from other minds, you are surrounded when in the negative orreceiving state. You are then as a sponge, unconsciously absorbing element, which may do great temporary harm or great permanent good to both mind and body.

During several hours of effort of any kind, such as talking business, walking, writing, or superintending your household, or doing any kind of artistic work, you have been positive, or sending out force. You have then to an extent drained yourself of force. If now you go immediately to a store crowded with hurried customers, or to a sick person, or a hospital, or a turbulent meeting, or to a trying interview with some disagreeable individual full of peevishness and quarrelsomeness, you become negative to them. You are then the sponge, drinking in the injurious thought element of the crowded store, the sickly thought element from the sick-bed or hospital, the actual poisonous and subtle element from any person or persons, whose minds put out a quality of thought less healthy or cruder than your own.

If you go fatigued in mind or body among a crowd of wearied, feverish, excited people, your strength is not drawn from you by them, for you have little strength to give. But you absorb, and, for the time being, make their hurried, wearied thought a part of yourself. You have then cast on you a load of lead, figuratively speaking. As you absorb their quality of thought, you will in many things think as they do and see also as they do. You will become discouraged, though before you were hopeful. Your plans for business, which, when by yourself, seemed likely to succeed, will now seem impossible and visionary. You will fear where before you had courage. You will possibly become undecided, and in the recklessness of indecision buy what you do not really need, or do something, or say something, or take some hasty step in business which you would not have done had you been by yourself, thinkingyour own thoughts, and not the clouded thoughts of the crowd around you. You will possibly return home fagged out and sick in mind and body.

Through these causes, the person whom you may meet an hour hence, or the condition of mind in which you are on meeting that person, may cause success or failure in your most important undertakings. From such a person you may absorb a thought which may cause you to alter your plans, either for success or failure.

If you must mingle among crowds, or with minds whose thoughts are inferior to your own, do so only when you are strongest in mind and body, and leave as soon as you feel wearied. When strong, you are the positive magnet, driving off their injurious thought-element. When weak, you become the negative magnet, attracting their thought to you; and such thought is freighted with physical and mental disease. Positive men are drivers and pushers, and succeed best in the world. Yet it is not well to be always in the positive or force-sending state of mind; if you are, you will divert from you many valuable ideas. There must be a time for the mental reservoir of force or thought to fill up as well as give forth. The person who is always in the positive attitude of mind--he or she who will never hear new ideas without immediately fighting them--who never takes time to give quiet hearing to ideas which may seem wild and extravagant, who insists ever that what does not seem reasonable to him must necessarily be unreasonable for every one else, such a mind will certainly, by constantly maintaining this mental attitude, be drained of all force.

On the other hand, the persons who are always negative or always in the receiving state, those who "never know their own minds" for two hours at a time, who are swayed unconsciously by everyone with whom they talk, who allow themselves, whenthey go with a plan or a purpose, to be discouraged by a sneer, by a single word of opposition, are as the reservoir, ever filling up with mud and trash, which at last stops the pipe for distributing water; in other words, they have their force-sending capacity almost destroyed, and are unsuccessful in everything which they undertake.

As a rule, you must be positive when you have dealings with the world, for very much the same reason that the pugilist must be positive when he stands before his antagonist. You must be negative when you retire from the ring--from active participation in business. You will tire yourself out by constantly confronting opponents, even in thought, in any sort of contest.

Why did the Christ of Judea so often withdrawfrom the multitude?It was because, after exercising in some way his Immense power of concentrated thought, either by healing or talking, or by giving some proofs of his command over the physical elements, at which times he was positive and expended his force, he, feeling the negative state coming upon him, left the crowd, so that he should not absorb their lower thought. Had he done so, his force would have been dissipated by carrying such thought, that is, by getting in sympathy with it, feeling it and thinking it, just as you may have done when a person, full of troubles, comes to you, and spends an hour telling those troubles to you, literally pouring into you his load of anxious thought. You sympathise, you are sorry, you desire strongly to help, and, when he leaves, your thought follows him. In such case, your own force is used up by the feeling of sympathy or sorrow, while it might otherwise have been applied to something far more beneficial and profitable in result both to yourself and him.

An orator would notspend an hour previous to his speech in public incarrying bushels of coal upstairs to relieve a tired labourer, for if he did, his strength, brilliancy, inspiration, the force required for his effort, would be mostly used up in the drudgery of carrying coal.The ideas which he puts forth may prove the direct or indirect means of relieving that labourer in some way, and even thousands of others.

You must be positive and restrain the outflow of your sympatheticforce very often in the cases of private individuals in trouble, in order to have power to do all the more for them. In politics and professions, the men who live longest and who exercise most influence are those who are least accessible to the masses; for if they are constantly mingling with all manner of people, and so absorbing varied atmospheres, much of their power is wasted in carrying it. Look at the long list of prominent American politicians who have died in the prime of life, or but little past it, during the last few decades; Seward, Grant, Morton, M'Clellan, Logan, Wilson, Hendricks, Chase, Stanton. Not keeping themselves positive--ignorant exposure to all manner of inferior thought atmospheres when negative--has been a most important factor in these premature deaths.

Great financiers like Jay Gould avoid the crowd and hubbub of the Stock Exchange. They live relatively secluded lives, are not easy of access, and transact much business through agents. In so doing, they avoid hurried and confused thought atmospheres. They surround and keep themselves as in a fortress, in the clearer thought-element of the world of finance, and from it derive their keensightedness on their plane of action. They realise the necessity of so doing without possibly being able to define the law. Many methods are quite unconsciously adopted by people which bring successful results in many fields of effort, and which are adopted through the unconscious action and teaching of the laws governing thought.

If you are now very much in the company of some person whose quality of thought is inferior to your own, you are certainly affected injuriously, through absorbing that person's thought since you cannot be positive all the time, to resist the entrance of his thought. When wearied, you are negative, or in a state for receiving his or her thought, and then it must act on you. As so it acts on you, unconsciously you may do many things, in conformity with his or her order of thought, which you would have done differently, and possibly better, had you not been exposed to it and absorbed it.

If so you absorb the element of fear or indecision from anyone, will you act in business with your own natural confidence, courage, energy and determination? It matters not what is the relation to you of those whose temporary or permanent association may thus do you harm, whether that of parent, brother, sister, wife or friend; if their mental growth is less than yours, and if therefore they cannot see as you see, you are very likely to be injured in mind, pocket and health through their constant association. For such reason, Paul the apostle advised people not to be "unequally yoked together in marriage." Why? Because he knew that of any two persons living constantly together, yet occupying different worlds of thought, one would surely be injured; and the one most injured is the highest, finest and broadest mind, which is loaded down, crippled and fettered by the grosser thought absorbed from the inferior.

If you are in active business sympathy or relation with any person who is nervous, excited, irritable, destitute of any capacity for repose, always worried about something, and on the rush from morning till night, though you are separated by hundreds of miles, you will, when in the receiving state, have that person's mind acting injuriously on yours, and you will have thereby sent to you much of his or hercruder thought-element, which, agitating and disturbing your mind, will, in time, work unpleasant results to the body.

Your only means of avoiding this is to cease such relation and common sympathy and effort with them as soon as possible,–to put them out of your mind,–to fix and interest yourself in some other diversion or occupation whenever your thought goes out to them. For every time that you so think, you send out your actual life and vitality in their direction, and thus doing you may transmit a current of life and force which will give them relative success in many undertakings, a success that you may lack, for you are transferring your capital stock of force, while you should use it for yourself. The cruder minds can only appropriate a part of this. The rest is wasted. They may be kept alive by it and prosper, and in return send you only element which brings on you disease, lack of energy and barrenness of idea.

Proper association is one of the greatest of agencies for realising success, health and happiness. Association here means something far beyond the physical proximity of bodies. You are literally nearest the person or persons of whom you think most, though they are ten thousand miles distant.

If you have been long in association with a person, so absorbing thought-element inferior to your own, you cannot, if you sever the connection, immediately free yourself from the inferior thought-current flowing from him to you, though thousands of miles may intervene. Distance amounts to little in the unseen world of thought. If such a person is much in your thought, his mind still acts on yours, sending you grosser and injurious element. You must learn to forget him if you wish to escape injury. That must be a gradual process. In so forgetting you cut the invisible wires binding you together, through which there have been sent elements injurious to you.

Does this sound cold, cruel and hard? But where is the benefit of two persons being so tied together in thought or remembrance, if one or both are injured? If one is injured so also must be the other in time. But the superior mind receives more immediate injury, and many a person fails to attain the position where he or she should stand, through this cause.

Through this cause also there come disease, lack of vigour, corpulency and clumsiness. The cruder element so sent you by another, and absorbed by you, can materialise itself in physical substance, and make itself seen and felt on your body in the shape of unhealthy and excessive fat, swollen limbs, or any other outward sign of disease and decay. In such case, it is not really your own unwieldy or deformed body that you are carrying about. It is the inferior body of another person sent you in thought; as year after year this process goes on, the cumbrous frame which you so carry becomes at last too heavy for your spirit, and then it drops off. You are "dead," in the estimation of your acquaintances, but you are not really dead; you have simply tumbled down under a load which you could no longer bear.

Even a book in which you are greatly interested, which draws strongly on your sympathy, and has much to say on the mental or physical distress of the person so drawing on your sympathy, can, if you read it in the negative or receiving state, bring to you some form of the physical or mental ailments alluded to therein. Such a book is the representative of the mind of the individual whose history it contains, acting on yours, and bringing to you in thought-element all that person's morbid and unhealthy states of mind, which for a time settle on you and become a parasitical part of you. In this way great harm may be done to sensitive people through reading novels and even true stories full of physical or mental suffering.

If a character to which you are stronglyattracted is described as being confined for years in a dungeon, suffering physical and mental pain from such confinement, and in the pages of that book if you follow such life and become absorbed in it, you do actually live therein. You will, if so reading such history day after day, and getting thoroughly absorbed or merged in it, find your vitality or your digestion affected in some way. The law operates, though you may never dream that the cold which you have taken more easily, through lack of vitality, the headache or weakness of digestion, is owing to a mental condition brought on you temporarily through living in the thought of that book while in the receiving state of mind. These are unhealthy books; and so are plays which work strongly on people's emotions in the dramatic representation of scenes of horror, distress and death. The health of thousands on thousands is injured through attracting and fastening on themselves, while in the negative or receiving condition, these unhealthy currents of thought and their consequent unhealthy mental states.

While eating, one should always be in the receptive condition, for then you are gathering material element to nourish the body; and if you eat in a calm, composed, cheerful frame of mind, you are receiving a similar character of thought. To eat and growl, to argue violently or intensely with others, to eat and still think business and plan business, is to be positive, when of all times you should then be negative. It is like working with your body while you eat. You send, while so arguing or grumbling, that force from you which is needed for digestion. It matters little whether you grumble or argue in speech or in thought.

There is also injurious result to you when any person at the table is for any reason--any offensive habit, any peculiarity of manner or mood-unpleasant to you, and you are thereby obliged toendure instead of enjoying his company, for all endurance means the putting out of positive thought-- in other words, working in mind to drive off the annoyance. Especially the dinner in the latter part of the day should be the day's climax of happiness--a union of minds in perfect accord with each other--the conversation light, bright, lively and humorous--the palates appreciative of artistic cookery, and the eye also regaled with the appointments of the table and the dining-room. In such a condition and in such receptive state you absorb a spiritual strength, coming from the thought of all about you as they will absorb yours. But if you eat in a social dungeon, in the barrack of a restaurant, where only material food is given, in an unhappy family, full of petty jealousies and complainings, in a boarding-house manger, you may exhaust yourself in resisting or enduring annoyances, thereby lessening the power of digestion and assimilation of your food; and you absorb also more or less of the discontent or moodiness of those about you, and so carry away a load worse than useless--a load which is the real cause of an imperfect digestion, of consequent physical weakness and mental unrest, or irritability.

When you are much alone, you attract and are surrounded by a quality and current of thought coming from minds similar to your own. It is for this reason, that in moments of solitude your thought may be more clear and agreeable than when in the company of others. You live then in another and finer world of ideas. You may deem these ideas but as " idle thoughts "; you may not dare to mention them before others; you may long for company, and may take such as you can get, or you may have it forced upon you. With it your ideal world is shattered, and seems possibly absolute nonsense. You enter into your neighbours' current of thought, their line of talk and motive. You chatter and run on asthey do; you criticise, censure, judge and possibly abuse others not present; when you are again by yourself, you feel a sense of discontent with yourself, and a certain vague self-condemnation for what you have been saying. That is your higher mind, your real self, protesting against the injury done itby the lower mind--or not possibly so much your lower mind as the lower thought which you absorb while in that company, and which for a time becomes a parasitical part of you, as the ivy-vine may fasten itself to the oak, from the root to the topmost branch, drawing its nourishment in part from the oak, giving it poison in return, and at last so covering it up that the tree is concealed and is eventually killed thereby.

In a similar manner are refined minds often buried, concealed and prevented their true expression by the lower and parasitical thought, which, unconscious of the evil it can do them, they enter among, associate with and allow to fasten upon them. They are not themselves, and perhaps from their earliest physical life never have been themselves, so far as outward expression goes. They are as oaks buried and concealed by the poisonous ivy. But you may say: "I cannot live alone and without association." True. It is not desirable or profitable that you should. It is not good for man or woman to live alone. It is most desirable, profitable and necessary that you should be fed by the strong, healthy, vigorous, cheerful thought-element coming from minds whose aspiration, ideal and motives are like your own.

When you cut off association or the flow even of your thought from those who are injurious to you, you prevent not only the intrusion of their evil quality of thought but you open the door for the better. You will then by degrees attract, in physical form, those who can give you at once more entertainment and more help. Your highest thought is an unseen force or link, ever connecting you with higherminds akin to your own. These cannot act on you to any extent so long as you continue association or are linked in thought with the lower. Such link or association bars the door to the higher.

How much real comfort, strength, cheer or entertainment do you get from your daily associates? Are they live company? Who does the entertaining, you or they?, who must ever keep up the conversation when it flags? Are you never bored by their prosiness, by all which you have heard over and over again, and if, when on hearing and rehearsing it you do not express discontent in your speech, do you not in your secret thought? How much of the association that you seek, or that seeks you, is really more endured than enjoyed, and is, in fact, only " taken up with " because of the lack of better.

You will never tire of your true and most profitable associates, who, having opened themselves to the higher, are ever drawing in new idea, and with this a new life, which they will give to you, as you give them in return. These are the "wells of water springing up unto everlasting life." These are the "savours of life unto life, and not of death unto death," as are minds to each other who, month after month and year after year, only think in a rut, talk in a rut and act in a rut. These are the dead who should be left to " bury their dead." True life is a state of continuous variety; it involves, through opening the mind in the right direction, and keeping it so open, an endless association with other and like minds, giving ever to each other, and receiving unfailing supply of strength, vigour and the elementsof eternal youth.

The fountain of youth, and endless youth, is a spiritual reality, as are many other things which are deemed idle vagaries, and have been erroneously sought on the physical stratum of life. The fountain of endless youth, youth of body as well as mind,lies in the attainment of that mental attitude or condition which is instantly positive to all evil, cruder and lower thought, but negative or receptive to higher and constructive thought, full of courage, devoid of all fear, deeming nothing impossible, hating no individual, disliking only error, full of love for all. but expanding its sympathy wisely and carefully.

Chapter 2
SOME PRACTICAL MENTAL RECIPES

NONE of us can expect to believe and live up to new laws, principles, or methods of life all at once. Though convinced of their truth, there is an unyielding, stubborn part of us which is hostile to them. That part is our material mind or mind of the body.

THERE IS A SUPREME POWER AND RULING FORCE WHICH PERVADES AND RULES THE BOUNDLESS UNIVERSE.

YOU ARE A PART OF THIS POWER.

YOU AS A PART HAVE THE FACULTY OF BRINGING TO YOU BY CONSTANT SILENT DESIRE, PRAYER, OR DEMAND MORE AND MORE OF THE QUALITIES, BELONGINGS, AND CHARACTERISTICS OF THIS POWER.

Every thought of yours is a real thing--a force (say this over to yourself twice).

Every thought of yours is literally building for you something for the future of good or ill.

What, then, Is your mind dwelling on now in any matter? The dark or the bright side? Is it toward others ugly or kind? This is precisely the same as asking, " What kind of life and results are you making for yourself in the future? "

If now you are obliged to live in a tenement house or sit at a very inferior table, or live among the coarse and vulgar, do not say to yourself that you must always so live. Live in mind or imagination in the better house. Sit in imagination at better served tables and among superior people. When you cultivate this state of mind your forces are carrying you to the better. Be rich in spirit, in mind, in imagination, and you will in time be rich in material things. It is the mood of mind you are most in, whether that be grovelling or aspiring, that is actually making physical conditions of life in advance for you.

The same law applies to the building up of the body. In imagination live in a strong, agile body, though yours is now a weak one.

Do not put any limits to your future possibilities. Do not say: "I must stop here. I must always rank below this or that great man or woman. My body must weaken, decay, and perish, because in the past so many people's bodies have weakened and perished."

Do not say: "My powers and talents are only of the common order and those of an ordinary person. I shall live and die as millions have done before me."

When you think this, as many do unconsciously, you imprison yourself in an untruth. You bring then to yourself the evil and painful results of an untruth. You bar and fetter your aspiration to grow to powers and possibilities beyond the world's present knowledge. You cut from you the higher truth and possibility.

You have latent in you, some power, some capacity, some shade of talent different from that ever before possessed by any human being. No two minds are precisely alike, for the Infinite Force creates infinite variety in its every expression, whether such expression be a sunset or a mind.

Demand at times to be permanently freed from all fear. Every second of such thought does its little to free you forever from the slavery of fear. The Infinite Mind knows no fear, and it is your eternal heritage to grow nearer and nearer to the Infinite Mind.

We absorb the thought of those with whom we are most in sympathy and association. We graft their mind on our own. If their mind is inferior to ours and not on the same plane of thought, we, in such absorption, take in and cultivate an inferior and injurious mental graft.

If you will keep company with people who are reckless and unaspiring, who have no aim or purpose in life, who have no faith in themselves or anything else, you place yourself in the thought current of failure. Your tendency then will be to failure. Because from such people, your closest associates, you will absorb their thought. If you absorb it, you will think it. You will get into the same mood of mind as theirs. If you think as they do, you will in many things find yourself acting as they do, no matter how great your mental gifts.

Your mind surely absorbs the kind of thought it is most with. If you are with the successful you absorb thought which brings success. The unsuccessful are ever sending from them thoughts of lack of order, lack of system, lack of method, or recklessness and discouraged thought. Your mind if much with theirs will certainly absorb these thoughts exactly as a sponge does water.

It is better for your art or business that you have no intimate company at all than the company of reckless, careless, slipshod, and slovenly minds.

When in your mind you cut yourself off from the unlucky and thriftless, your body will not long remain so near theirs. You get then into another force or current. It will carry you into the lives of more successful people.

When you don't know what to do in any matter of business, in anything--wait. Do nothing about it. Dismiss it as much as you can from your mind. Your purpose will be as strong as ever. You are then receiving and accumulating force to put on that purpose. It comes from the Supreme Power. It will come in the shape of an idea, an inspiration, an event, an opportunity. You have not stopped while you so waited. You have all that time been carried to the idea, the inspiration, the event, the opportunity, and it also has been carried or attracted to you.

When in any undertaking we put our main dependence and trust in an individual or individuals and not in the Supreme Power, we are off the main track of the most perfect success.

The highest and real success means, in addition to wealth, increasing health, vigour, and a growth never ceasing into powers and possibilities not yet realised by the race.

As regards your business, don't talk to anybody, man or woman, regarding your plans or projects, or anything connected with them, unless you are perfectly sure they wish for your success. Don't talk to people who hear you out of politeness. Every word so spoken represents so much force taken out of your project. The number you can talk to with profit is very small. But the good wish of one real friend, if he give you a hearing but for ten minutes, is a literal, living, active force, added to your own, and from that time working in your behalf.

If your aim is for right and justice you will be led to those you can trust and talk to with safety. Your spiritual being or sense will tell you whom you can trust.

When you demand justice for yourself, you demand it for the whole race. If you allow yourself to be dominated, brow-beaten, or cheated by others without inward or outward protest, you are condoning deceit and trickery. You are in league with it.

Three persons engaged in any form of gossip, tattle, or scandal generate a force and send it from them of tattle, gossip, and scandal. The thought they send into the air returns to them and does them injury in mind and body. It is far more profitable to talk with others of things which go to work out good. Every sentence you speak is a spiritual force to you and others for good or ill.

Ten minutes spent in growling at your luck, or in growling at others because they have more luck than yourself, means ten minutes of your own force spent in making worse your own health and fortune. Every thought of envy or hatred sent another is a boomerang. It flies back to you and hurts you. The envy or dislike we may feel toward those who, as some express it, " put on airs," the ugly feeling we may have at seeing others riding in carriages and "rolling in wealth,' represents just so much thought (i. e. force) most extravagantly expended, for in its expenditure we get not only unhappiness but destroy future fortune and happiness.

If this has been your common habit or mood of mind, do not expect to get out of it at once. Once you are convinced of the harm done you by such mood, a new force has come to gradually remove the old mind and bring a new one. But all changes must be gradual.

Your own private room is your chief workshop for generating your spiritual force and building yourself up. If it is kept in disorder, if things are flung recklessly about, and you cannot lay your hands instantly upon them, it is an indication that your mind is in the same condition, and therefore your mind as it works on others, in carrying out your projects, will work with less effect and result by reason of its disordered and disorganised condition.

Ill-temper or despondency is a disease. The mind subject to it in any degree a sick mind. The sick mind makes the sick body. The great majority of the sick are not in bed.

When you are peevish, remember your mind is sick. Demand then a well mind.

When you say to yourself, "I am going to have a pleasant visit or a pleasant journey," you are literally sending elements and forces ahead of your body that will arrange things to make your visit or journey pleasant. When before the visit or the journey or the shopping trip you are in a bad humour, or fearful or apprehensive of something unpleasant, you are sending unseen agencies ahead of you which will make some kind of unpleasantness.

Our thoughts, or in other words, our state of mind, is ever at work " fixing up " things good or bad for us in advance.

As you cultivate this state of mind more and more you will at last have no need of reminding yourself to get into such mood. Because the mood will have become a part of your everyday nature, and you cannot then get out of it, or prevent the pleasant experiences it will bring you.

Our real self is that which we cannot see, hear, or feel with the physical senses--our mind. The body is an instrument it uses. We are then made up entirely of forces we call thoughts. When these thoughts are evil or immature they bring us pain and ill-fortune. We can always change them for better thoughts or forces. Earnest steady desire for a new mind (or self) will surely bring the new mind and more successful self. And this will ever be changing through such desire for the newer and ever more successful self.

All of us do really "pray without ceasing." We do not mean by prayer any set formality or form of words. A person who sets his or her mind on the dark side of life, who lives over and over the misfortunes and disappointments of the past, prays for similar misfortunes and disappointments in the future. If you will see nothing but ill luck in the future, you are praying for such ill luck and will surely get it.

You carry into company not only your body, but what is of far more importance, your thought or mood of mind, and this thought or mood, though you say little or nothing, will create with others an impression for or against you, and as it acts on other minds will bring you results favourable or unfavourable according to its character.

What you think is of far more importance than what you say or do. Because your thought never for a moment ceases its action on others or whatever it is placed upon. Whatever you do has been done because of a previous, long held mood or state of mind before such doing.

The thought or mood of mind most profitable in permanent results to you is the desire to do right. This is not sentiment, but science. Because the character of your thought brings to you events, persons, and opportunities with as much certainty as the state of the atmosphere brings rain or dry weather.

To do right is to bring to yourself the best and most lasting result for happiness. You must prove this for yourself.

Doing right is not, however, doing what others may say or think to be right. If you have no standard of right and wrong of your own, you are acting always on the standard held or made by others.

Your mind is always working and acting on other minds to your advantage or disadvantage whether your body is asleep or awake. Your real being in the form of a thought travels like electricity through space. So when you lay the body down to sleep, see that your mind is in the best mood to get during your physical unconsciousness the best things. For if you go to sleep angry or despondent your thought goes straight to the unprofitable domain of anger or despondency, and will bring to your physical life on awakening, first the element and afterwards that ill success which anger and despondency always attract.

Health is involved in the Biblical adage, " Let not the sun go down on your wrath." Every mood of mind you get into brings to you flesh, bone, and blood of a quality or character like itself. People who from year to year live in moods of gloom or discouragement are building elements of gloom and discouragement into their bodies, and the ill results cannot be quickly removed.

The habit of hurry wears out more bodies and kills more people than is realised. If you put on your shoes hurriedly while dressing in the morning you will be very apt to be in a hurry all day. Pray to get out of the current of hurried thought into that of repose. Hurried methods of doing business lose many thousands of dollars. Power to keep your body strong and vigorous--power to have influence with people worth holding--power to succeed in your undertakings comes of that reposeful frame of mind which while doing relatively little with the body, sees far ahead and clearly in mind.

So, when in the morning, be you man or woman, you look at what is to be done and begin to feel yourself overwhelmed and hurried by the household cares, the writing, the shopping, the people to be seen, the many things to be done, sit right down for thirty seconds and say, " I will not be mobbed and driven in mind by these duties. I will now proceed to do one thing--one thing alone, and let the rest take care of themselves until it is done." The chances are then that the one thing will be done well. If that is done well, so will all the rest. And the current of thought you bring to you in so cultivating this mood will bear you to far more profitable sur-roundings, scenes, events, and associations than will the semi-insane mood and current of hurry.

All of us believe in many untruths today. It is an unconscious belief. The error is not brought before our minds. Still we go on acting and living in accordance with our unconscious error, and the suffering we may experience comes from that wrong belief.

Demand, then, every day ability to see our wrong beliefs. We need not be discouraged if we see many more than we think we have at present. They cannot be seen and remedied all at once.

Don't take a " tired feeling " or one of languor in the day time for a symptom of sickness. It is only your mind asking for rest from some old rut of occupation.

If your stomach is disordered make your mind responsible for it. Say to yourself, " This disagreeable feeling comes of an error in thought." If you are weak or nervous, don't lay the fault on your body. Say again, "It is a state of my mind which causes this physical ailment, and I demand to get rid of such state and get a better one." If you think any medicine or medical advice will do you good, by all means take it, but mind and keep this thought behind it: " I am taking this medicine not to help my body but as an aid to my spirit,"

Your child is a mind which having lost the body it used in a past physical existence (and possibly of another race and country), has received a new one, as you did in your own infancy.

Tell your child never to think meanly of itself. For if it becomes habituated to such thought, others will feel it and think of the child first and of the grown-up person afterwards as of small value.

Nothing damages the individual more than self-deprecation, and many a child Is weighted down with the elements of failure before it goes into the world through years of scolding, snub-bing, and telling it that it is a worthless being.

Tell your child in all its plans to see or think only success. To keep in the permanent mood of expecting success, brings causes, events, and opportunities, which bring success.

Let us also tell this to ourselves very often, for we are but children also, with physical bodies a few years older than the infants.

We have as yet but the vaguest idea of what life really means, and the possibilities it has in store for us. One attribute of the relatively perfected life to come to this race is the retention or preservation of a physical body so long as the mind or spirit desires it. It will be a body also free from pain and sickness, and one which can be made or unmade, put on or taken off, at will.

Say of anything that "it must be done" and you are putting out a mighty unseen power for doing. When your mind is in the mood of ever saying "must," whether you have in mind the particular thing you aim at or not, still that force is ever working on your purpose. But we need to be careful as to what that force of "must" is put on. "Must" without asking for wisdom as to where it shall be placed may bring you terrible results.

Always in your individual aims and purposes defer to the Higher Power and Infinite Wisdom. The thing you may most desire might prove a curse. Be always, then, in the mood of saying,

"There is a Power which knows what will bring me the most permanent happiness better than I do. If my desire is not good let it not come, for in its place I shall have something better."

If you send your thought in sympathy to everyone who calls for it, you may have very little left to help yourself. It is necessary to have great care in the choice of those on whom we put our love and thought. One may help build us up; another tear us down. We need to ask for wisdom that we may know whom to receive in close association.

As you are a part of God or the Supreme Power, and a peculiar part, you can always estimate yourself as the very best of such peculiar part. No one else can approach or equal or excel you, as you represent and put out your own peculiar powers, gifts, or shades of mind and character. You will in time command the world of your own mind, and while others may compel your admiration, you will do yourself a great injury if you worship them or abase yourself or grovel before them even in mind.

Idolatry is the blind worship of anything or any body save the Infinite Force from which alone you draw life, power, and inspiration.

The thought of a woman coming to you, or a man, in sympathy or love, with ideas, aims, and aspirations equal to or above yours, may prove to you a source of strength of muscle, health of body, and clearness of mind. His or her thought so flowing to you is a real element. If a man or woman inferior to you mentally is your companion or much in your thought, your mind will be much less clear and your health will eventually suffer.

Be you man or woman, your life cannot be complete and you cannot build yourself rapidly into higher and higher powers until you meet and recognise spiritually your eternal complement or completement in the other sex. And from such complement there is no departure.

When we eat and drink let us remember that with every mouthful we place and build a thought into our selves in accordance with the mood we are in while eating. So be sure to be bright, hopeful, and buoyant while eating, and if you cannot command such mood of mind, pray for it. To ask night and morning of the Supreme Power for the highest wisdom (that is, the greatest good and happiness), and to demand this in that frame of mind which acknowledges the

superiority of that Wisdom over your own, is certainly to put yourself in the current of the greatest and most enduring health and prosperity. Because another and better current of thought then begins to act on you and will gradually carry you out of errors and into the right. It will lead you by degrees into different surroundings, different ways of living, and will in time bring you the association you really need and what is best for you.

Chapter 3
SELF-TEACHING; OR, THE ART OF LEARNING HOW TO LEARN

IT is a commonly received opinion, that in youth it is easier to learn than in after years; that at "middle age," or after, the mind becomes, as it were, set in a rut or mould, which does not readily receive new impressions. This idea is expressed in the adage: "You can't teach an old dog new tricks."

People have made this a truth by accepting it as a truth. It is not a truth. If your mind is allowed to grow and strengthen, it will learn more easily and quickly than during the infancy of the body. It will learn more and more quickly *how*, to learn any new thing. Learning *how* to learn, learning how to grasp at the principles underlying any art, is a study and a science by itself.

The child, in most cases, does not learn so quickly as many suppose. Think of the years often spent at school, from the age of six to sixteen or eighteen, and how little, relatively, is learned during that period. But this time of life is not regarded as of so much importance as that after eighteen or twenty. He or she would be deemed to have a dull intellect, who should require fourteen years to gain only so much as what a large proportion of children gain from the age of six to twenty.

It is possible for any man or woman whose mind has grown to that degree, that they can acknowledge that every possibility exists within themselves to learn any art, any profession, any business, and become skilled therein, and this even without teachers, and at the period termed "middle age," or after, providing,

First, That they are in living earnest to learn.

Second, That they fight obstinately against the idea of " can't," or that they are too old to learn.

Third. That in all effort to become proficient in their new calling, they cease such effort as soon as it becomes fatiguing or irksome, and that they make of such effort a recreation, and not a drudgery.

Fourth, That they allow no other person to argue, sneer, or ridicule them out of the truth that the human mind can accomplish anything it sets its forces persistently upon.

Fifth, That they keep their minds in the attitude of ever desiring, demanding, praying for whatever quality or trait of character or temperament they need to succeed in their effort; and that whenever the thought of such effort is in mind, it shall be accompanied with this unspoken thought: "I will do what I have set out to do."

There should be no "hard study" at any age. Real "study" is easy and pleasing mental effort; as when you watch the motion of an animal that awakens your curiosity, of a person that interests you. You are studying when you admire and examine the structure of a beautiful flower; you are studying the method and style of an actor or actress when they most hold and compel your attention and admiration. All admiration is in reality study. When you admire anything that is beautiful, your mind is concentrated upon it. You are quite unconsciously examining it. You remember, without effort, many of its features, or characteristics. That unforced examination and attention is study.

To "study hard " is to try to admire; to try to admire is to try to love; to try to love, or to be forced by others to try to love, generally ends in hating the thing or pursuit so forced upon you,–one reason why so often the schoolboy hates "to learn his lesson."

The experience of those who have gone before us in any art, trade, occupation, or profession, is unquestionably valuable, but valuable only as suggestion. There is a great deal laid down as rules and "canons of art" which shackle and repress originality. The idea is constantly, though indirectly, impressed on learners, that the utmost limit of perfection has been reached in some art by some " old master," and that it would be ridiculous to think of surpassing him.

Now, genius knows no "old master." It knows no set form of rules made for it by others. It makes its own rules as it goes along, as did Shakespeare, Byron, and Scott in literature, and the first Napoleon in war; and your mind may have in it the seed of some new idea, discovery, invention, some new rendering of art in some form, which the world never saw before.

Any man or woman who loves to look at trees and flowers, lakes and rivulets, waves, waterfalls, and clouds, has within him or her the faculty for imitating them in the effects of light, shade, and colour,–has, in brief, a taste for painting.

You say, "People to be artists, must have the art born within them." I say, " If they admire the art, they have within them the faculty for advance in that art."

You say, " But because I admire a rose, or a landscape, it is no sign I can ever paint either." I say, "Yes, you can, providing you really want to.

But how! Put your effort on it for an hour, half an-hour, fifteen minutes, a day. Begin. Begin anywhere. Anything in this world will do for a starting point. Begin, and try to imitate on paper a dead leaf, a live one, a stone, a rock, a log, a box, a brickbat. A brickbat lying in the mud has lying with it light, shade and colour, and the laws governing them, as much as a cathedral, and is a better foundation than a cathedral to begin on. Begin with the stub of a pencil, on the back of an old envelope. Every minute of such work after beginning is so much practice gained. Every minute before such beginning, providing you intend to begin, and do not, is so much practice lost, as regards that particular art.

Mind, however, you make of such practice a recreation, just as boys do in ball throwing and catching, or as the billiard player does who takes up the cue for half-an-hour, matched only against himself, or as the horseman does who exercises the horse for practice before the race. When the work becomes irksome, when you get out of patience, because your brickbat won't come out on the paper like the original, drop it, wait for your patience-reservoir to fill up, and take for your next copy a log, a tree trunk, or anything else.

You say that you should go to a teacher of this or that art, so that you can become " properly grounded in its principles," and that, by such teacher's aid, you shall avoid blundering and stumbling along, making little or no progress.

Take up any trade, any handicraft, any art, all by yourself, and grope along in it by yourself for a few weeks, and at the end of that time you will have many well-defined and intelligent questions to ask about it, of someone more experienced in it than yourself,–the teacher. That is the time to go to the teacher. The teacher should come in when an interest in the art or study is awakened. To have him before, is like answering questions before they are asked.

You cannot teach a dog to paint. The intelligence using the dog's organisation has not grown to an appreciation of such imitation of natural objects. But you can teach him to draw a cart, to "point" to game in the cover, to swim out to the water-fowl you have shot, and bring it to you. Why? Because the dog has these instincts, or desires, born in him. The trainer, his teacher, brings them out. Some men and women have no more admiration for a beautiful landscape than the dog. Of course, neither can ever be taught to paint, because they have not the desire to paint, nor the admiration of the thing to be painted.

"Then, whatever a man or woman really desires to do, is to be taken as some proof that they can do it? " you ask. "Yes; that is the exact idea." *Desire to accomplish is a proof of ability to accomplish.* Of course, such ability may be weighted down and kept back by many causes, such as ill-health of body, ill-health of mind, unfavourable surroundings, and, perhaps, greatest of all, utter ignorance that such desire is a proof of the possession of power to accomplish the thing desired.

How did you learn to walk, and how did you learn to talk? Could anyone have taught you, if desire to walk and talk had not been born with you? Did you go to a walking teacher, or a talking teacher? Did you not learn both accomplishments after ten thousand failures? So far as you can remember, was it not rather an amusement than otherwise, to learn both, or at least, was there any idea of work associated with these early efforts?

You place a boy or girl by the water-side, and give them full liberty, and they will learn to swim as naturally as they learn to walk, because the desire to swim is in them. If, after learning, they see a better swimmer, they will naturally try to imitate him; and all this endeavour, from first to last, will be for them far more recreation than work. The better swimmer who comes along represents the teacher; and the boy and girl who can already swim fairly well, and are anxious to swim better, represent pupils who are in a condition to be taught.

Think for a moment, how much it was necessary to teach your body in training it to walk. First, to balance yourself upright on two feet without falling. Secondly, to balance yourself on one foot without falling. Thirdly, to move the body. Fourthly, to give it the direction in which you wanted to go. And yet we call walking a "mechanical," and not a mental, effort.

If you are determined to paint, and love the creations of nature and art well enough to try and imitate them, you will be constantly studying effects in light and shade on rocks, stones, cliffs, towers, steeples. You will observe and study, and be rejoiced at the many changing aspects and colours of the sky, as you never were before. You will discover, as you continue to observe, that nature has a different shade of colour for every day of the year, and almost every hour of the day. You will suddenly find in all this a new and permanent recreation, without money and without price. You will then find new interests and new sources of amusement in studying the works of painters and their methods, which will be revealed to you just so fast as your appreciation *grows* up to them.

The same principle will apply to any branch of mechanics or art,–to anything. Of course, it is best to pursue that for which you have the most inclination, that is, admiration. If you are in any occupation that does not suit you, and you want to engage in some art that does suit you, if you have fifteen minutes in the day to spare, begin on that art.

If it is painting, paint a brickbat in some idle moment as well as you can, and only as a means of amusement. If it is carving, you have always the means for practice, if you have a jack-knife and a bit of wood. If it be music, a banjo or guitar with but a single string will give you means for practice. For you must commence in the simplest way, even as you crept before you walked. There must be imperfect effort before there can be relatively perfect result.

Because, when you do so begin, you begin to practise with one instrument far more ingenious and complicated than any you can buy for use in your art; namely, your mind.

If we begin in this way, we begin something else; we begin drawing toward us ways, means, helps, and agencies unseen, but powerful, to help us. We are not to expect success in an hour, a day, a month, a year. But if we persist, a relative success is coming all the while. The effort of this month is better than that of last. There may come periods of weariness and discouragement; periods when, as we look back, we seem to have made no advance; periods, in fact, when we seem to have gone back, when we seem to be doing worse than at the start; periods when we lose all interest in the work. It makes us sick to look at it, even to think of taking it up again; and a certain sense of guilt at our neglect intensifies the sickness.

That is a mistake. If, in our music, our painting, our profession, our business, be it what it may, we strive for some certain result, and fail, time after time, and week after week, to effect it, yet we are still advancing towards it.

We may not see such advance. That is because the advance is not in the direction we think it should be. There may be a screw loose in a part of our mental being that we have taken no note of, which keeps us back. That screw, in very many cases, lies in the state of mind in which we take up our work or pursuit.

We may be too anxious or impatient. We take up the pen, the brush, or the tool, in a hurried frame of mind. We want to do too many things at once. Or we endeavour to crowd the doing of several things in too short a limit of time. Or we are unable to dismiss all thought, save what bears on the effort now in hand.

All such moods are destructive to the best effort. They take much of our force from that effort. A common result is that we can do nothing to suit us. We throw down our work in disgust. We may not take it up again for weeks. We do take it up at last, perhaps, in a listless, indifferent frame of mind. We do not then set our hearts on doing anything perfect, or making it come up to our ideal in a moment, and that Is the very time when we produce some new effect; when we hit the idea we have aimed at; when we are surprised at the apparently accidental development of a new power within us.

There is a great mystery in this,–a mystery we may never solve,–the mystery that whatever purpose this power within us we call mind sets itself upon, fixes itself upon persistently, that purpose it is accomplishing, that purpose it is carrying out, that purpose it is ever drawing nearer to itself, not only when we work for it with the body and the intellect; we are also *growing ever towards it when it seems for the time forgotten,* or when we are asleep.

That persistent purpose, that strong desire, that never-ceasing longing, is a seed in the mind. It is rooted there. It is alive. It never stops growing. Why this is so, we may never know. Perhaps it is not desirable to know. It is enough to know that it is so. There is a wonderful law involved in it. This law, when known, followed out, and trusted, leads every individual to mighty and beautiful results. This law, followed with our eyes open, leads to more and more happiness in life; but followed blindly, involuntarily with our eyes shut, leads to misery.

To succeed in any undertaking, any art, any trade, any profession, simply keep it ever persistently fixed in mind as an aim, and then study to treat all effort towards it as play, recreation. The moment it becomes "hard work," we are not advancing. I mean by "play," that both body and mind work easily and pleasantly. It matters not what a man or woman is doing, whether digging sand or scrubbing floors, when the mind is interested in that work and the muscles are full of strength, such work is play, and is more apt to be well done. When the muscles are exhausted of their power, and will alone drives the body forward, the occupation soon becomes work, drudgery, and is much the more apt to be ill done. I begin low down in illustration, as low as sand, mud, brickbats; but the principle is the same, be the worker a hod-carrier or a Michael Angelo.

The science of learning to learn, then, involves largely that of making recreation of all effort. This is not as easy as it may seem. It involves a continual prayer for patience, patience, patience.

"Patience to play?" you ask. Yes. When we are amused by any effort of our own, be it effort of the eye, in seeing sights that please it, or effort of the ear, in hearing sounds that please it, or effort of muscle in exercising them, that is the very time when we are most attentive and most absorbed. The very time when we forget there is such a thing as patience, is the very time we most exercise patience.

That is the mood we need to cultivate. Because moods of mind determine the character and quality of effort. The painter writes out his mood in his picture; a mistake, a blur, a defect, a daub, may write out in that picture too much hurry to get ahead. He took up his brush, possibly, full of irritation, because his wife asked him for more money for household expenses; result, he puts a woman in that picture twelve feet high as proportioned to other objects, when she should have been but four. What put on that extra and needless eight feet? A mood born of household expenses. Or the scrubber wrote out her mood of mind on the floor. Where? In that neglected corner, where the last dust of summer lingers alone. Why? Because her mood of hurry to be through with her work is there written; or her mood of dishonesty, in doing as little as possible for the money to be received; or her mood of anxiety concerning the sick child, left at home in some squalid tenement; or the poor woman's mood born of physical weakness, in thus trying to do a man's work, with no nutritious food in her stomach, and no money to buy any till the work is done.

My very practical friend, you who despise all "art flummery," all and everything that is not "business," and smells of wood, or stone, or leather, or bank-bills, this cultivation of the mood is of vast importance to you, also; because, when you meet your brother Hard Cash, to have a wrangle over bargain and sale, the man who is in the coolest mood, the most collected mood, the mood most free of other thought, or care, the man who is in the least hurry, the man who throws overboard all anxiety as to results, the man who is not too eager, who can lie back in his chair and make a joke or laugh at you, when millions are trembling in the balance, who keeps all his reserve force till it is needed, that is the man who can play the best hand in your game, and make the best bargain. That is the man who gains his end by some knowledge of spiritual law; and spiritual law can be used for all purposes, and purposes relatively low as well as high; and in some things the wicked, so-called, of today, are better informed in certain phases of spiritual law than those who call themselves good.

How shall we get ourselves, then, into the most desirable mood for doing our best? By praying for it, asking for it, demanding it, in season and out of season. We can wish an earnest desire in a second, no matter where we are. That is a prayer. It is a thought that goes out, and does its work in bringing us another atom of the quality desired. That atom is never lost. It adds itself to and adds its strength to all the other atoms of the same quality so gained. So you call this simple? Is the method too easy? Remember, we are indeed fearfully and wonderfully made; and when Solomon wrote this he had an inkling of the existence of powers wrapped up in human bodies, that startled him, and would us, did we more fully realise them.

Possibly this question may be asked: "What is the use of cultivating, or encouraging others to cultivate any form of art, when for thousands the struggle is so hard today for bread?" Or, in other words, " What is the use of educating people to wants and desires they cannot satisfy?" Or, " What bearing and benefit has art cultivation in righting the 'great wrongs' of the hour?"

It is of the greatest possible benefit. Art, art appreciation, art cultivation, refines human nature. Refinement demands finer surroundings, finer food, finer houses, cleaner houses, cleaner clothes, cleaner skin. You can't make people clean, neat, tasteful, by telling them they "ought" to be so. They must have brought out of them some calling, some occupation, some work which will implant ever-increasing desire for more of the elegancies of life. Much of what is called the
"oppression" of the strong over the weak, the rich over the poor, comes because so many of the poor do not aspire above a pig-pen under the window, a mud-puddle in the back-yard, and a front garden growing tomato cans, dead cats, and old hoop-skirts. Much of the money today given in charity to the poor, is really poured from one rich man's pocket into that of another, and relieves only a temporary distress.

You roll half a ton of coal this winter into the poor man's cellar. His family are warmed for the hour. The profits go into the safe of the coal corporation. Its heat warms human beings with little ambition above animals. You encourage that man's boy or girl to paint ever so roughly with the cheapest of water-colours, to mould forms in clay, to have any faculty awakened which shall show them what a beautiful world they really live in, and soon with this there may come a growing distaste for the mud-puddle in the back-yard, and the display of hoopskirts and tomato cans in the front. Show these children that they have within them more or less of this mighty and mysterious element--mind, and that through its exercise they can become almost anything to which they aspire, and that the more of the Infinite Spirit they call to themselves, the more will the have to strengthen, beautify, enrich, invigorate, and electrify their souls and bodies, and you have then started them on the road of doing for themselves, by the powers in themselves. They are then on a road leading away from both charitable soup-kitchens and gin-shops.

If they cultivate the love of grace and beauty in any direction, they cultivate also an ability for expressing such grace and beauty. If they follow the law of persistent demand for improvement in such grace or beauty, whether it be by the exercise of pen or tongue, of painting or sculpture, or self-command, or polish of manner, or the art of actor, elocutionist. musician, or worker on stone, worker in metal, cultivator of plant, tree, flower, they will at last do something a *little better* than anyone else can do, in their peculiar way, and through their self-taught, peculiar method; and when they can do this, the world will gladly come to them, and bring them its dollars and cents, for what they can please it with.

None of us know what is in us till we try to bring it out; A man, or woman, may go their whole life with some wonderful power, some remarkable talent which would benefit and please mankind, feeling it ever from time to time, struggling for expression in a desire to use it, in a longing to express it, yet having it ever forced back by that fatal thought, "I can't."

"It's no use." " It's ridiculous, the idea of my aspiring to such a thing." We are treasure boxes, holding wondrous powers. We brought these treasures with us into the world from an immeasurably far-off past--a past we may not compute--a past the spirit, born into being, the tiniest atom, the faintest movement, drawing to itself ever, age after age, through unconscious exercise of desire or demand, more and more of power, more and more of complex organisation, more and more of variety of talent, more and more of the marvellous power coming through combination and re-combination of element, until at last the man is born, the woman is born, blind at first, blind as millions now are regarding the wealth within them; blind to faith and belief in themselves, until the veil is pulled from their eyes, and then they shall soon spring up into gods, destined to a career of eternal life, eternal growth, and eternal and illimitable happiness.

Chapter 4
LOVE THYSELF

CHRIST'S Precepts say: " Love thy neighbour as thyself." Some people incline to forget the two last words "as thyself," and infer that we should love others even better than ourselves. So far has this idea been carried that it has led in cases to entire sacrifice and neglect of self so that good may be done to others. There is a justifiable and righteous love for self. There can be no true spiritual growth without this higher love for self. Spiritual growth implies the cultivation and increase of every faculty and talent. It means the making of the symmetrically developed man and woman. Spiritual growth, fostered by unceasing demand of the Supreme Power, will bring power to keep the body in perfect health--so as to escape pain and disease--and will eventually carry man above the present limited conditions of mortality. The higher love of self benefits others as well as ourselves.

When we love a person, we send that person our quality of thought. If it is the aspiring order of thought, it is for that person a literal element and agency of life and health in proportion to his or her capacity for absorbing and assimilating it. If we think meanly of ourselves--if we are beggarly in spirit--and are content to live on the bounty of others, if we care little for our personal appearance --if we are willing to get money by questionable means--if we believe there is no Supreme and overruling Power, governing our lives by an exact law, but that everything is left to chance, and that life is only a scramble for existence, we send in thought such beliefs to that person, and if our love is accepted it is only a means to drag down instead of a power to elevate.

How can we send the highest love to another if we do not have it for ourselves? If we are careless and unappreciative of the body's great use to us--if we never give it a thought of admiration or gratitude for the many functions which it performs for us --if we regard it with the same indifference that we may have for the post to which we hitch a horse, we shall send that same quality of sentiment and thought to the person of whom we think most, and the tendency will be to generate a similar disregard for themselves. Either they will do this, or seeking light of the Infinite, they will find themselves obliged in self-protection to refuse the love which we send them, because of its coarser and grosser quality. This is sometimes the error of mothers, who say: " I don't care for myself so that my son or daughter's welfare is assured. I give and devote my whole life to them."

This means: "I am content to grow old and unattractive, I am content to slave and drudge so that my children may receive a good education and shine in society. I am an old and decaying weather-beaten hulk and can't hold together much longer; the best use which I can make of myself is to serve as a sort of foot-bridge for them in the shape of nurse, grandmother and overseer of the nursery and kitchen, while they are playing their parts in society." The daughter receives this thought with the mother's inferior, self-neglecting love. She absorbs and assimilates it. It becomes part of her being. She lives it, acts it out, and thirty years afterwards is saying and doing the same and laying herself upon the shelf with the rest of the cracked teapots for her own daughter's sake.

Ancestral traits of character, as bequeathed and transmitted from parent to child, are the thoughts of the parent absorbed by the child. When in thought, desire and aspiration we make the most of what the Infinite has given us (inclusive of these wonderful bodies), we shall have continual increase, and such increase will overflow of its own accord and benefit others. The highest love for self means justice to self. If we are unjust to ourselves, we shall be unavoidably unjust to those to whom we are of the greatest value. A general who should deprive himself of necessary food and give all his bread and meat to a hungry soldier, might in so doing weaken his body, and with his body weaken his mental faculties, lessen his capacity for command, thereby increasing the chances for the destruction of his entire army.

What is most necessary to know, and what the Infinite will show us if we demand, is the value which we are to others. In proportion to our power for increasing human happiness, and in proportion as we recognise that power, will the needful agencies come to us for making our material condition more comfortable. No man or woman can do their best work for themselves or others who lives in a hovel, dresses meanly and starves the spirit by depriving it of the gratification of its finer tastes. Such persons will always carry the atmosphere and influence of the hovel with them, and that is brutalising and degrading. If the Infinite worked on such a basis, would the heavens show the splendour of the suns? Would the fields reflect that glory in the myriad hues of leaf and flower, in plumage of bird and hue of rainbow?

What in many cases prevents the exercise of this higher love and justice to self is the thought; "What will others say, and how will others judge me, if I give myself what I owe to myself?" That is, you must not ride in your carriage until every needy relative has a carriage also. The general must not nourish his body properly because the hungry soldier might say that he was rioting in excess. When we appeal to the Supreme and our life is governed by a principle , we are not actuated either fear of public opinion or love of others' approbation, and we may be sure that the Supreme will sustain us. If in any way we try to live to suit others, we shall never suit them; the more we try, the more unreasonable and exacting do they become. The government of your life is a matter which lies entirely between God and yourself; when your life Is swayed and influenced from any other source you are on the wrong path.

Very few people really love themselves. Very few really love their own bodies with the higher love. That higher love puts ever-increasing life in the body and ever-increasing capacity to enjoy life. Some place all their love on the apparel which they place on their bodies; some on the food they put in their bodies; some on the use or pleasure they can get from their bodies. That is not real love for self which gluts the body with food or keeps it continually under the influence of stimulants. It is not a real love for self which indulges to excess in any pleasure to be obtained from the body. The man who racks and strains his body and mind in the headlong pursuit of pleasures or business, loves that business or art unwisely. He has no regard for the instrument on which he is dependent for the materialisation of his ideas. This is like the mechanic who should allow a costly tool, by which he is enabled to do rare and elaborate work, to rust or be otherwise injured through neglect. That is not the highest love for self which puts on its best and cleanest apparel when it goes out to visit or promenade and wears ragged or soiled clothes indoors. That is love of the opinion or approbation of others. Such a person only dresses physically. There is a spiritual dressing of the body when the mind in which apparel is put on is felt by others. Whoever has it in any degree will show it in a certain style of carrying his clothes which no tailor can give.

The miser does not love himself. He loves money better than self. To live with a half-starved body, to deny self of every luxury, to get along with the poorest and cheapest things, to deprive self of amusement and recreation in order to lay up money, is surely no love for the whole self. The miser's love is all in his money-bags, and his body soon shows how little love is put in it. Love Is an element as literal as air or water. It has many grades of quality with different people. Like gold, it may be mixed with grosser element. The highest and purest love comes to him or her who is most in communion and oneness with the Infinite Mind, is ever demanding of the Infinite Mind more and more of its wisdom. The regard and thought of such persons is of great value to anyone on whom it is directed. And such persons will, through that wisdom, be wisely economical of their sympathy for others and put a great deal of this higher love into themselves in order to make the most of themselves.

Some people infer from their religious teachings that the body and its functions are inherently vile and depraved; that they are a clog and an encumbrance to any higher and more divine life; that they are corruptible "food for worms," destined to return to dust and moulder in the earth. It has been held that the body should be mortified, that the flesh should be crucified and starved and subjected to rigorous penance and pains for its evil tendencies. Even youth, with its freshness, beauty, vigour and vivacity, has been held as almost a sin, or as a condition especially prone to sin. When a person in any way mortifies and crucifies the body, either by starving it, dressing meanly, or living in bare and gloomy surroundings, he generates and literally puts in the body the thought of hatred for itself. Hatred of others or of self is a slow thought-poison. A hated body can never be symmetrical or healthy. The body is not to be refined and purged of the lower and animal tendencies being made responsible and continually blamed these sins--by being counted as a clod and an encumbrance, which it is fortunate at last to shake off.

Religion, so-called, has in the past made a scapegoat of the body, accused it of every sin, and, in so doing and thinking, has filled it with sin. As one result, the professors of such religion have suffered pain and sickness. Their bodies have decayed, and death has often been preceded by long and painful illness. " By their fruits ye shall know them." The fruits of such a faith and condition of mind prove error therein.

There is a mind of the body--a carnal or material mind--a mind belonging to the instrument used by the spirit. It is a mind or thought lower or crude than that of the spirit. But this mind of the body need not, as has been held, be ever at war with the higher mind of the spirit. It can, through demand of the Infinite, be made in time to act in perfect accord with the spirit. The Supreme Power can and will send us a supreme love for the body. That love we need to have. Not to love one's body is not to love one expression of the Infinite Mind.

We are not inferring that you "ought" to have more than reasonable love for your body, or that you "ought" in any respect to do or act differently from your deeds, acts and thoughts as they are at present. Regarding others, "ought " is a word and idea with which we have nothing to do. There is no reason in saying to a blind man: "You ought to see." There is no more reason in saying to anyone: " You ought not to have this or that defect of character." Whatever our mental condition may be at present, that we must act out. A man cannot, of his individual self, put an atom more of the element of love in himself than he now has. Only the Infinite Mind can do that. Whatever of in character and belief we have today, we shall act out today in thought or deed. But we need not always have that mind.

The Overruling Mind will, as we demand, give us new minds, new truths, new beliefs, and as these supplant and drive out old errors there will come corresponding changes for the better, in both mind and body. And these ever-improving changes have no end. There is to these changes but one gate, as there is but one road. That gate and road lie in an unceasing demand of the Infinite to perfect us in Its way.

"There is a natural body, and there is a spiritual body." In other words, we have a body of physical element which can be seen and felt, and we have another body which is intangible to our physical senses. When we are able to love, cherish and admire our physical body as one piece of God's handiwork, we are putting such higher love-element not only into that physical body but also into the spiritual body. We cannot of ourselves make this quality of love. It can come to us only through demand of the Infinite. It is not vanity or that lower pride which values more whatever effect its own grace and beauty may have on others than it values that grace and beauty. The higher love for the body will attend as carefully to its external adornment in the solitude of the forest as it would in the crowded city. It will no more debase itself by any vulgar act in privacy than it would before a multitude.

God gives one personal beauty and symmetry in physical proportions, should not he or she, thus favoured with a gift from the Supreme, admire these endowments? Is it vanity to love and seek to improve and increase any talent which we may find in ourselves? If God made man and woman " in His own image," is it an image to be loved and admired, or regarded with hatred and distrust? Why, the religious belief of less than a hundred years ago actually courted ugliness, and inferred that it was more creditable than beauty. Had some of those solemn-visaged professors been delegated to make an angel after their own ideal, they would have turned out a duplicate of themselves.

The Infinite, as we demand, will give us wisdom and light to know what we owe to ourselves. People have been over-ridden with the idea of their duties to parent, relative or friend. The road to heaven has been marked out as one full of sacrifice and self-denial for the sake of others, and of little good or pleasure for self. If Christ should be taken as an example in this respect, we find a very different course inferred. When charged with lack of attention to his mother, he asked; "Who is my mother?" When the young man pleads, as an excuse for not immediately following Christ, that filial duty demanded he should go and bury his father, the Messenger of a new and higher law said: "Let the dead bury their dead." In other words: If father or mother or sister or brother are steeped in a lifelong course of trespass and sin--if their lives have been one continual violation of spiritual law, bringing the inevitable penalty of disease and pain--if they are hardened and fossilised in their false beliefs, and regard your opinions as visionary and impractical you cannot, without injury, have fellowship with them. If you pretend for the sake of peace to agree with them, you are living a lie, and when you act or live a lie you materialise it and put it in your body, where it is a breeder of pain and unrest.

If others cannot see the law of life as clearly as you, and in their blindness go stumbling on and filling themselves with decay and disease, it is not in the line of the highest justice that you should be called on to nurse them every time that they are sick, to absorb their sick and unhealthy thought, to give them your life and vitality (for this you do when you think much of any one), and to be dragged down with them. You are not responsible for their blindness, nor can you open their eyes and make them see what is proven to you to be truth. Only the Infinite can do that. You do those who are in this lower and material current of thought no real good in ministering to them physically or spiritually. You may, having the stronger mind, bolster them up for a time, and, throwing your mind in theirs, you may give them your strength, but you cannot do this always, and when your influence is removed, as some time it must be, they will fall back to their old condition. What then have you accomplished You have taken so much force out of yourself that you owed to yourself; you have taught them to depend on you and not on what everyone must learn to depend on--the Supreme Power. Let the dead then, who are still above ground, bury their dead. Give them a thought and wish for their highest welfare whenever you do think of them, but leave them in God's care.

When you put the Higher Love into yourself --when you reserve your forces to raise yourself higher in the scale of being--when it is your aim and unceasing, silent prayer to be raised out of the current of the lower and material thought into that spiritual condition beyond the reach of physical disease--when you aspire to have every sense and faculty refined and strengthened beyond the present lot of mortals--when you begin to realise, through the proofs coming to you, that these are possibilities, then you are a real benefit to everyone. You are then proving a law. You are showing that there is a road out of the ills which afflict humanity, and when others, seeing these things evidenced in your own life, ask how you obtain them, you can reply: " I have grown, and am ever growing, into a higher and happier condition of mind and body, through knowledge of a law, and that law is as much for you to live by as for me." You may be able to say: " I believe in the existence of the Great Overruling Power which will show me ever the happier way of life as I demand wisdom of that Power. I had little faith in the existence of that Power at first, but I was prompted to pray or demand ability to see its reality. Now my faith in its reality is growing firmer."

To throw our whole being, care and thought into the welfare of others, no matter who they may be, without first asking of the Supreme if it be the wisest thing to do, is a sin, for it is an endeavour to use the forces given us by that Power as we think best. The result is damage to self and a great lessening of ability to do real good to others. Between the Supreme Mind and ourselves there should exist a love which is at once a love of ourselves and a love of that Mind. We must love what we draw from it, since what we draw and make part of self is drawn from God, and is a part of God. Every thought which we give to the Supreme Wisdom enriches us and directs us in the lasting path of happiness. Every thought which we give to others who are not actuated by the Higher Wisdom is unwisely bestowed. That Wisdom will direct our thought, love and sympathy to those on whom it can be bestowed without injury. To have our thoughts ever flowing spontaneously toward the Infinite Mind is to be one with God and a wise lover of self, as we feel ourselves more and more parts of God manifest in the flesh.

If we give sympathy and aid, material or moral, to others as they call for it, and without reservation or judgment, people will take all that we have to give and come open-mouthed for more. They will keep this up until we are exhausted. No outsider will put a limit to your giving. You must do that yourself. What is called "generous impulse" is sometimes another name for extravagance and injustice to somebody. Those who fling money to servitors and overpay largely for trifling services often owe that money to others, or they may owe it to themselves. In the really spiritual domain of being, we find this injustice perpetrated. on a still larger scale. Sympathetic natures sometimes give their whole lives to others. Giving thus their life and force to others becomes a fixed habit. They grow unable to restrain or control their sympathy. It overflows at everybody's call. They deprive themselves of things really needed and take up with the poorest in order to satisfy a mania for the squandering of time, force, effort and thought on others. A widely spread idea prevails that we can never give too much or do too much for others. It argues that salvation is more readily attained by such reckless expenditure of self than in any other way. No matter how barren it makes our lives--no matter of how much we deprive ourselves, it is to be made up to us tenfold in time.

We deem this a great mistake. We believe there is a Divine Economy which orders that when we give even our thought, we must give only as much as will really benefit others. Reckless prodigality throws dollars to children when cents would do them as much good. Reckless prodigality of sympathy (force) often gives ten times more to a person than that person can appropriate. What people cannot appropriate is lost for them, and when you have sent it once out you cannot recall it.

Undoubtedly to some, the idea of giving so much love to self will seem very cold, hard and unmerciful. Still this matter may be seen in a different light, when we find that "looking out for Number One," as directed by the Infinite, is really looking out for Number Two and is indeed the only way to permanently benefit Number Two. The gifts conferred by the Supreme Power are "perfect gifts," and a "perfect gift" once received by us goes out and benefits many others. So soon as one person on this planet receives the "perfect gift" of immortality in the flesh, involving perfect health and freedom from all pain and disease, that gift will be contagious, for health is catching as well as disease. The cornerstone of all symmetrical growth and constant increase of mental and physical power is the reservation and care of our thought-forces. This wisdom can only come as we demand it of the Supreme Power.

I am often asked: " How do you know what you assert? " Or: " Have you proved these assertions to yourself?" I know what I assert to be true, because I have seen its beneficial results as regards health and condition in life made evident. Other proofs are constantly coming. But what is clear to me is really no permanently convincing demonstration to any other person. That kind of proof you can only get from yourself and by the exercise and growth of your share of power given you by the Infinite. In the physical world we can safely accept the statement of a navigator who asserts his discovery of a new island. The island looks the same to every physical eye. But on the spiritual side of life spiritual things do not appear the same to all eyes. There are, so to speak, spiritual islands and spiritual realities which one person can see and another cannot see. You will see and get proof of these in proportion as you grow, and very possibly when you tell these things to others, they will call you a visionary, or will ascribe the material proof of such growth to some material cause. In the spiritual life every person is his or her own discoverer, and you need not be grieved if your discoveries are not believed in by others. It is not your business to argue and prove them to others. It is your business to push on, finding more and increase of your own individual happiness. Christ said to those of his time: "Though one rose from the dead you would not believe him." In this respect the world has not much changed since Christ used a material body on Earth.

Chapter 5
THE ART OF FORGETTING

IN the chemistry of the future, thought will be recognised as substance even as the acids, oxides and all other chemicals of today.

There is no chasm betwixt what we call the material and spiritual. Both are of substance or element. They blend imperceptibly into each other. In reality the material is only a visible form of the finer elements which we call spiritual.

Our unseen and unspoken thought is ever flowing from us, an element and force, real as the stream of water which we can see, or the current of electricity which we cannot see. It blends with the thought of others, and out of such combination new qualities of thought are formed, as in the mixture of chemicals there are formed new substances.

If you send from you in thought the elements of worry, fret, hatred or grief, you are putting in action forces that are injurious to your mind and body. The power to forget implies the power of driving the unpleasant and hurtful thought or element, and bringing in its place the profitable element, to build up instead of tearing us down.

The character of thought which we think or put out affects our business favourably or unfavourably, It influences others for or against us. It is an element felt pleasantly or unpleasantly by others, inspiring them with confidence or distrust.

The prevailing state of mind, or character of thought, shapes the body and features. It makes us ugly or pleasing, attractive or repulsive to others. Our thought shapes our gestures, our mannerism, our walk. The least movement of muscle has a mood of mind, a thought, behind it. A mind always determined has always a determined walk. A mind always weak, shifting, vacillating and uncertain, makes a shuffling, shambling, uncertain gait. The spirit of determination braces every nerve and sinew; the thought-element of determination fills every muscle.

Look at the discontented, gloomy, melancholy and ill-tempered men or women, who manifest in their faces the operation of the silent force, which is their unpleasant thought, cutting, carving and shaping them to their present expression. Such people are never in good health, for that force acts on them as poison, and creates some form of disease. A persistent thought of determination on some purpose, especially if such purpose be of benefit to others as well as ourselves, will fill every nerve with strength. It is a wise selfishness that works to benefit others along with ourselves. In spirit, and in actual element, we are all united. We are forces which act and re-act on each other, for good or ill, through what ignorantly we call "empty space." There are unseen nerves extending from man to man, from being to being. Every form of life is in this sense connected together. We are all "members of one body." An evil thought or act is a pulsation of pain thrilling through myriads of organisations. The kindly thought and act have the same effect for pleasure. It is, then, a law of nature and of science that we cannot do a real good for another without doing one also to ourselves.

To grieve at any loss, be it of friend or property, weakens mind and body. It is no help to the friend grieved for. It is rather an injury; for our sad thought must reach its object, even if passed to another condition of existence, and is a source of pain to that person.

An hour of grumbling, fret, or fear, whether spoken or silent, uses up so much element or force in making us less endurable to others, and perhaps making for us enemies. Directly or indirectly, it injures our business. Sour looks and words drive away good customers. Grumbling or hating is a use of actual element to belabour our minds. The force which we may so expend could be put to our pleasure and profit, even as the force we might use with a club to beat our own body can be employed to give us comfort and recreation.

To be able, then, to throw off (or forget) a thought or force which is injuring us, is a most important means of gaining strength of body and clearness of mind. Strength of body and clearness of mind bring success in all undertakings.

They bring also strength of spirit; and the forces of our spirits act on others whose bodies are thousands of miles distant, for our advantage or disadvantage. The reason is that there is a force belonging to all of us, separate and apart from that of the body. It is ever in action, and ever acting on others. It must be in operation at each moment, whether the body be asleep or awake. Ignorantly, unconsciously and hence unwisely used, it plunges us into mires of misery and error. Intelligently and wisely used, it will bring us every conceivable good.

That force is our thought. Every thought of ours is of vital importance to health and true success. And so-called success, as the world terms it, is not real. A fortune gained at the cost of health is not a real success.

Every mind trains itself, generally unconsciously, to its peculiar character or quality of thought. Whatever that training is, it cannot be immediately changed. We may have trained our minds unconsciously to nourish evil or troubled thought. We may never have realised that brooding over disappointment, living in a grief, dreading a loss, fretting for fear this or that might not succeed as we wish, was building up a destructive force which has bled away our strength, created disease, unfitted us for business, and caused us loss of money and possibly loss of friends.

To learn to forget is as necessary and useful as to learn to remember. We think of many things every day which it would be more profitable not to think of at all. The ability to forget is the ability to drive away the unseen force (thought) which Is injuring us, and to change it for a force (or order of thought) which can benefit us.

Demand imperiously and persistently any quality of character in which you may be lacking, and you will attract increase of such quality. Demand more patience or decision, more judgment or courage, more hopefulness or exactness, and you will increase in such qualities. These qualities are real elements. They belong to the subtler, and as yet unrecognised, chemistry of Nature.

The discouraged, hopeless and whining man has unconsciously demanded discouragement and hopelessness. So he gets it. This is his unconscious mental training for evil. Mind is "magnetic," because it attracts to itself whatever thought it fixes itself upon, or that to which it opens itself. Give space to fear, and you will fear more and more. Cease to resist its tendency, make no effort to forget it, and you open the door and invite fear in; you then demand fear. Set your mind on the thought of courage, see yourself in mind or imagination as courageous, and you will become more stout of heart. You demand courage.

There is no limit in unseen nature to the supply of these spiritual qualities. In the words: "Ask
and ye shall receive," the Christ implied that any mind could, through demanding, draw to itself all that it needed of any quality. Demand wisely, and we draw to us the best.

Every second of wise demand brings an increase of power. Such increase is never lost to us. This is an effort for lasting gain that we can use at any time. What all of us want is more power to work results, and build up our fortunes,–power to make things about us more comfortable, to ourselves and our friends. We cannot feed others if we have no energy to keep starvation from ourselves. The power to do this is a different thing from the power to hold in memory other people's opinions, or a collection of so-called facts gathered from books, which time often proves to be fictions. Every success in any grade of life has been accomplished through spiritual power, through unseen force flowing from one mind, working on other minds far and near, and as real as the force in your arm which lifts a stone.

A man may be illiterate, yet he may send from his mind a force affecting and influencing many others, far and near, in a way to benefit his fortunes, while the scholarly man drudges with his brain on a pittance. The illiterate man's is then a greater spiritual power. Intellect is not a bag to hold facts. Intellect is power to work results. Writing books is but a fragment of the work of intellect. The greatest philosophers have planned first, and acted afterwards, as did Columbus, Napoleon, Fulton, Morse, Edison and others, who have moved the world, besides telling the world how it should be moved.

Your plan, purpose or design, whether relating to a business or an invention, is a real construction of unseen thought-element. Such thought-structure is also a magnet. It commences to draw aiding forces to it so soon as made. Persist in holding to your plan or purpose, and these forces come nearer and nearer; they become stronger and stronger, and will bring more and more favourable results.

Abandon your purpose, and you stop the further approach of these forces, destroying also so much of unseen attracting power as you have already built up. Success in any business depends on the application of this law. Persistent resolve on any purpose is a real attractive force or element, drawing constantly more and more aids for carrying out that resolve.

When your body is in the state called sleep, these forces (your thoughts) are still active. They are then working on other minds. If your last thought before sleep is that of worry, of anxiety, of hatred for anyone, it will work for you only ill results. If it is hopeful, cheerful, confident and at peace with all men, it is then the stronger force, and will work for you good results. If the sun goes down on your anger, that wrathful thought will act on others, while you sleep, and bring only injury in return.

Is it not a necessity, then, to cultivate the power of forgetting what we wish, so that the current which attracts the ill, while our body rests, shall be changed to the current which attracts the good alone? Today thousands on thousands never think of controlling the character of their thought. They allow their minds to drift. They never say of a thought that is troubling them: "I won't think of it." Unconsciously then they demand what works them ill, and their bodies are made sick by the kind of thought on which they allow their minds to fasten.

When you realise the injury done you through any kind of troubled thought, you will then commence to acquire the power of casting it aside. When in mind you commence to resist such injurious thought, you are constantly gaining more and more power for resistance. "Resist the devil," said the Christ, " and he will flee from you." There are no devils save the ill-used forces of the mind. But these are most powerful to afflict and torture us. An ugly or melancholy mood of mind is a devil. It can make us sick, lose us friends, and lose us money. Money means the enjoyment of necessities and comforts. Without these we cannot do or be our best. The sin involved in " love of money" is to love money better than the things needful which money can bring.

To bring to us the greatest success in any business, to make the greatest advance in any art, to further any cause, it is absolutely necessary that at certain daily intervals we should forget all about that business, art or cause. By so doing we rest our minds, and gather fresh force for renewed effort.

To be ever revolving the same plan, study or speculation, what we shall do or shall not do, is to waste such force on a brain-treadmill. We are in thought saying to ourselves the same thing over and over again. We are building of this actual, unseen element, of this thought, the same constructions over and over again. One is a useless duplicate of the other.

If we are always inclined to think or converse on one particular subject; if we will never forget it; if we will start it at all times and in all places; if we will not in thought and speech fall into the prevailing tone of the conversation about us; if we do not try to get up an interest in what is being talked of by others; if we determine only to converse on what interests us, or not converse at all, we are in danger of becoming "cranks" or monomaniacs.

The "crank" draws his reputation on himself. He is one who, having forced one idea, and one alone, on himself, has resolved, perhaps unconsciously, to foist that same idea on everybody else. He will not forget at periods his pet theory or purpose, and adapt himself to the height of others. For this reason he loses the power to forget, to throw from his mind the one absorbing thought. He drifts more and more into that one idea. He surrounds himself with its peculiar atmosphere, or element, and it becomes no less real than any other which we can see or handle.

Others near him feel the influence of this single idea, and feel it disagreeably, because the thought of one person is felt by others near him through a sense as yet unnamed. In the exercise of this sense lies the secret of your favourable or unfavourable "impressions" of people at first sight. You are in thought, as it flows from you always, sending into the air an element which affects others for or against you, according to its quality, and in proportion to the acuteness of their sense which feels thought. You are influenced by the thought of others in the same way, be they far or near. Hence we are talking to others when our tongues are still. We are making ourselves hated or loved while we sit alone in the privacy of our chambers.

A crank often becomes a martyr, or thinks himself one. There is no absolute necessity for martyrdom in any cause, save the necessity of ignorance. There never was any absolute necessity, save for the same reason. Martyrdom always implies lack of judgment and tact in the presentation of any principle new to the world. Analyse martyrdom, and you will find in the martyr a determination to force on people some idea in an offensive and antagonistic form. People of great ability, through dwelling on one idea, have at last been captured by it. The antagonism which they drew from others they drew because they held it first in their own mind.

"I come not to bring peace," said the Christ, "but a sword." The time has now come in the world's history for the sword to be sheathed. Many good people unconsciously use swords in advising what they deem better things. There is the sword (in thought) of the scolding reformer, the sword of dislike for others because they won't heed what you say, and the sword of prejudice because others won't adopt your peculiar habits. Every discordant thought against others is a sword, and calls out from others a sword in return. The thought which you thus put forth is the thought that you receive back, and it is therefore after the same kind.

The coming empire of peace is to be built up by reconciling differences, making friends of enemies, telling people of the good that is in them rather than the bad, discouraging gossip and evil-speaking by the introduction of subjects more pleasant and profitable, and proving through one's life that there are laws, not generally recognised, which will give health, happiness and fortune, without injustice or injury to others. Its advocate will meet the sick with the smile of true friendship, for the most diseased people are always the greatest sinners. The most repulsive man or woman, the creature full of deceit, treachery and venom, needs your pity and help of all the most, for that man or woman, through generating evil thought, is generating pain and disease for himself or for herself.

You are thinking of a person unpleasantly from whom you have received some slight or insult, an injury or injustice. Such thought remains with you hour after hour, perhaps day after day. You become at last tired of it, yet cannot throw it off. It annoys, worries, frets, sickens you. You cannot prevent yourself from going round on this same tiresome, troublesome track of thought. It wears out your spirit; and whatever wears the spirit, wears also the body.

This is because you have drawn on yourself the other person's opposing and hostile thought. He is thinking of you, as you are of him. He is sending you a wave of hostile thought. You are both giving and receiving the blows of unseen elements. You may keep up this silent war of unseen force for weeks and, if so, both are injured. This contest of opposing wills and forces is going on all about us. The air is full of it.

The struggle to forget enemies, or to throw out to them only friendly thought, is then as much an act of serf-protection as to put up your hands and ward off a physical blow. The persistent thought of friendliness turns aside thought of ill-will, and renders it harmless. The injunction of Christ to do good to your enemies is founded on a natural law. It is saying that the thought or element of good will carries the greater power, and will always turn aside and prevent injury coming from the thought of ill-will.

Demand forgetfulness when you can only think of a person or of anything with the pain that comes of grief, anger or any other cause. Demand is a state of mind which sets in motion forces to bring you the result needed. Demand is the scientific basis of prayer. Do not supplicate. Demand persistently your share of force out of the elements about you, by which you can rule your mind to any desired mood.

There are no limits to the strength which may be gained through the cultivation of our thought- power. It can keep from us all pain arising from grief, from loss of fortune, loss of friends, and disagreeable situations in life. Such power is the very element or attitude of mind most favourable to the gain of fortune and friends. The stronger mind throws off the burdensome, wearying, fretting thought, forgets it, and interests itself in something else. The weaker mind dwells in the fretting, worrying thought, and is enslaved thereby. When you fear a misfortune (which may never happen), your body becomes weak; your energy is paralysed. But you can, through constantly demanding it, dig out of yourself a power which will throw off any fear or troublesome state of mind. Such power is the high road to success.

Demand it, and it will increase more and more, until at last you will know no fear. A fearless man or woman can accomplish wonders.

That no individual may have gained the full height of this power, is no proof that it cannot be really gained. Newer and more wonderful things are ever happening in the world. Some decades ago, and he who should assert that a human voice could be heard between New York and Philadelphia would have been called a lunatic. Now, the wonder of the telephone is an everyday affair. The powers, still unrecognised, of our thought will make the telephone of trivial importance. Men and women, through cultivation and use of this power, are to do wonders which fiction dares not or has not put before the world.

Chapter 6
SPELLS; OR, THE LAW OF CHANGE

A CONDITION Of mind can be brought on you, resulting to you in good or ill, sickness or health, wealth or poverty, by the action, conscious or unconscious, of other minds about you, and also through the thought suggested to you by objects or scenes about you.

This is the secret of what in former times was called the "spell." Through the action of thought a state of mind can be brought on any person which may make them act conformably to such thought.

The "spell" is a matter of everyday occurrence in some form or other. To remain for an hour in sight of grand scenery casts on the mind a "spell" of pleasurable thought. To remain for an hour in a vault surrounded by coffins and skeletons would, through the associations connected with such objects, cast on you a "spell" of gloom. To live for days and weeks in a family, all of whose members hated you, or were prejudiced against you, would most likely cast on you a spell of depression and unpleasant sensation. To live in a family whose members were always sending you warm and friendly thought would produce a " spell" of pleasurable sensation.

If, when sick, you are obliged to remain for days and possibly weeks in the same room, your mind will become weary of seeing continually the same objects in it. Not only is the mind wearied at sight of these objects, but the sight of each one, from day to day, will suggest the same train of thoughts. which also soon becomes wearisome. Mind weariness, from this or any other cause, has a natural drift towards despondency. Matters present and future then assume their darkest aspect and the darkest side of every possibility comes uppermost. Despondent thought, as has been many times repeated, is force used to tear the body down instead of building it up.

This action and condition of thought is one form of the "spell." It is broken most speedily by a change to another place and another room.

For this reason "change of scene" is frequently recommended to the invalid. Change of scene and locality means not only a change of objects beheld by the eye but a change also in thought, as new ideas, and possibly a new condition of mind, come through seeing the new set of objects. The new condition of mind will "break the spell."

There is a much closer connection between things tangible and seen of the eye and things intangible than is generally imagined. In other words, there is a close connection between things material and thing spiritual.

The force or element which we call " thought" is all-pervading, and takes innumerable varieties of expression. A tree is an expression of thought as well as a man, and so are all that we call inanimate objects.

There is not a thoroughly dead or inanimate thing in the universe, but there are countless shades of life or animation. Many things seem dead to us, as a bone or a stone, but there is a life or force which has built that bone or stone into its present condition, and that same life or force, after that bone or stone has served a certain purpose, will take it to pieces again and build its elements into other forms. The unbuilding process we call decomposition. It matters not if the stone change or rid itself of but one atom in a thousand years. Time is nothing in the working of Nature's forces. Decomposition, then, is a proof of the existence of all-pervading and ever-working life or force. Otherwise, the stone or bone would remain without change through all Eternity. Incessant change is ever going on in the boundless universe; it is an Inevitable accompaniment of all life; and the greater the life and force in you, the more rapid and varied will be the changes.

Everything, from a stone to a human being, sends out to you, as you look upon it, a certain amount of force, affecting you beneficially or injuriously according to the quantity of life or animation which it possesses.

Take any article of furniture, a chair or bedstead, for instance. It contains not only the thought of
those who first planned and moulded it in its construction, but it is also permeated with the

thought and varying moods of all who have sat on it or slept in it. So also are the walls and every article of furniture in any room permeated with the thought of those who have dwelt in it, and if it has been long lived in by people whose lives were narrow, whose occupation varied little from year to year, whose moods were dismal and cheerless, the walls and furniture will be saturated with this gloomy and sickly order of thought.

If you are very sensitive, and stay in such a room but for a single day, you will feel in some way the depressing effect of such thought, unless you keep very positive to it, and to keep sufficiently positive for twenty-four hours at a time to resist it would be extremely difficult. If you are in any degree weak or ailing you are then most negative or open to the nearest thought- element about you, and will be affected by it, in addition to the wearying mental effect, first mentioned, of any object kept constantly before the eyes.

It is injurious, then, to be sick, or even wearied, in a room where other people have been sick, or where they have died, because in thought-element all the misery and depression, not only of the sick and dying but of such as gathered there and sympathised with the patient, will be still left in that room, and this is a powerful unseen agent for acting injuriously on the living.

Those "simple savages" who after a death burn not only the habitation but every article used by the deceased when alive, may know more of Nature's injurious and beneficial forces than we know. Living more natural lives, they unconsciously act according to the law, even as animals in their wild and natural state do, thereby escaping many of the pains and discomforts of the artificial life which we have made both for ourselves and the animals that we domesticate.

People who have some purpose in life, who travel a great deal, who are ever on the move and in contact with different persons and places, have, you will notice, more vitality, more energy, and physically preserve a certain freshness not evident with those who follow year after year an unvarying round of occupation, carrying them day after day to one certain locality, whether office or desk or workman's bench, just as a pendulum oscillates from side to side.

These last look older at forty than the active, changing person does at sixty, because their unvarying lives, the daily presence and sight of the same objects at their dwellings or places of business, contact with the same individual or individuals at meals and in leisure moments, and interchange of about the same thoughts year in and year out, weave about them an invisible web composed of strands or filaments of the same unvarying thought, and this web literally strengthens from year to year, exactly as strand after strand of wire laid together will form at last the massive bridge-supporting cable. But the unseen cable so made binds people more and more firmly to the same place, the same occupation, and the same unvarying set of habits. It makes them dislike more and more even the thought of any change. It is another form of the "spell" which they have woven for themselves. It is the sure result of always keeping your state of mind unchanged.

We do not live on bread or meat alone. We live also largely on ideas. The person ever planning and moving new enterprises, the person who throws his force into beneficial pub- lic movements, and from either of these causes is led into a varied and ever-changing contact with individuals, receives and puts out a far greater variety of thought than the man who lives continually in a nutshell.

There is a time and use for retirement and solitude. There is a time and use for contact with the world. It is desirable to establish the golden mean between the two.

The person whose range of life and movement is narrow, who is doing nearly the same thing and seeing nearly the same things and people from year to year, has a tendency to feed mostly on the same old set of thoughts and ideas. Out of himself he generates the same order of old, stale notion and expression. Start him in a certain train of idea or association and he tells you time after time the same old story, forgetting how many times he has told it you before. He has about the same forms of expression for every occurrence and every hour of the day. He regards the world and things generally as about worn out. Lacking in life and variety of thought himself, he regards everything else as lacking in life and variety. For life is to us exactly as we see it through the spectacles which we so often unconsciously make to look at it. If our mental spectacles, through living unaware in violation of the Law, are blurred, cracked, discoloured, and dim, the whole world will to us seem blurred, discoloured, and dull in hue.

Such a person "ages," as we term it, very rapidly, because his physical body is as much an expression of his daily and prevailing order of thought as the apple is an expression or part of the apple tree. Feeding and living on the same set of ideas continually is analogous fo feeding continually on a most limited variety of food. Both bring on disease. In some of the English prisons what are called "oatmeal sores" afflict the prisoners through being fed so much on that single article.

But the average mental condition shows itself on the body far more rapidly than any result from material diet. It is feeding on the same stale set of ideas, aided by living continually amid the same physical surroundings and with the same individuals, who are likewise subsisting mentally on the same stale mental diet, that whitens the hair, stoops the shoulders, wrinkles the face, and causes shrinkage of tissues and bodily inertia and weakness. Our land is full of people who at forty-five, through this cause, look older than others of sixty-five. It is full also of young men and women in a physical sense, who, through their poverty of idea and lack of real life, will be old, worn, and haggard within twenty years. They are in substance as much old fogies, "grannies," and "daddies" now as are those whom they ridicule as such. They are travelling in the same narrow rut of idea. Slang phrases and worn-out chaff, borrowed from others, constitute four- fifths of their talk and probably five-sixths of their thought.

To this class also belong many who are deemed of a high order intellectually, or of more "culture," whose thought after all is very largely a repetition of what they have heard or read, who look up to and idolise some human authority, living or dead, and have really very few ideas of their own, not possibly because new ideas occasionally do not suggest themselves to them, but they have not the courage to secretly entertain and familiarise themselves with such ideas. They smother them. They succeed at last in killing them and putting out the little light endeavouring to shine on them. When you destroy or so kill out of yourself the capacity for truthful idea to act upon you, you are killing also your body by degrees. You are cutting off the only source of new life for the body.

Of this order of minds the only claim to youth lies in that physical freshness belonging to the earlier growth and life of the body, which, owing to their mental condition, will fade in twenty years as surely as the absence of sunshine and water will soon wither the young and growing plant.

Such are now unconsciously weaving for themselves the web and "spell" of age and decay.

A constant renewal of physical life lies only in a never-ceasing change of mental conditions. New ideas beget newer and fresher views of life. There are millions on millions of truthful, new ideas ready to come to us, provided we keep the mind in the proper state to receive them. We have not to plod and "study hard" to receive them. There is no "hard study" in the kingdom of God or the kingdom of infinite good. If in the line of communication with that kingdom, we shall ever receive new thought, as the plant receives the sunshine and air, and like the plant just as much as suffices to give us life for the day and the hour. Every mind is now, or is to be at some period of its existence (not possibly in this present physical existence), a fountain for the reception of such new idea.

But new thought cannot come from books or from the ideas of others. These may for a time serve to start you on the road, or as temporary props or helps. But if you depend altogether on books or people for new thought, you are living on borrowed life. You, in so doing, keep your own mind closed to the inflowing of the element which its own individual needs call for, which is for it alone and for no other mind. You must draw your own sustenance from the infinite reservoir of truthful thought. Until you do so you are not a "well of water springing up into everlasting life," nor have you reached the initial point of that real and perfected existence which feels at home anywhere in the universe and can draw its self-sustaining life at any place in the universe.

No agency fetters more or does more harm to both mind and body than a very close and constant association with a mind or minds inferior to yours in tastes, in refinement, in breadth of views and quality of motive.

Such order of mind ever near you and with which you are much in sympathy, will infuse into yours more or less of its grosser desire or taste. It will blind you more or less to higher and healthier views and modes of life. You will, unconsciously to yourself, live and act out much of that mind's life. You will be peevish or cynical or mean in your dealings, when it is not the real you that is so thinking or acting, but the constant flow to you and reception by you of the grosser force or element of that mind, which you thus act out. You become, then, literally a part of the other and inferior mind. This will surely affect the body which in its material substance becomes a material expression of that lower mind grafted on yours. Unless you sunder this mental tie, the inferior graft may outgrow the original tree. You will become physically inert, lifeless, and be affected with some form of disease, because you are then giving that inferior graft your own thought or force. It can appropriate but a small part of that force, but from what it can, it draws its own stinted life. You are then giving of your gold and getting base metal in return. You are then giving of your life and getting a slow and living death in return. For the mind most clear and active in thought, considerate, wise and prudent, broadly but not recklessly benevolent in action, does give to others, and especially to those with whom it is in close sympathy, life and vigour, both of mind and body.

Talking openly has very little to do with the good or ill results coming of minds in close association and sympathy. It is not what people talk. It is what people *think* of each other that most affects them. A person always near you and ever thinking of you with dissatisfaction or peevishness, or putting out the thought of opposition to your aims and wishes, will eventually make you feel unpleasantly, be his or her words ever so fair. Such a person, under these circumstances, will at last injure you in mind and body. That person is throwing a "spell" on you.

On the contrary, the near presence of a person pleasantly disposed toward you, who wishes to bring you pleasure or benefit without "an axe to grind," will give you a feeling of rest and quiet, though such person may not say a word for hours. These different sensations are among the many proofs that thought is a literal element, in some way ever affecting us, and ever bringing results as it comes to us from others or is sent by us to others. In this last case the "spell" may be beneficial to you.

There is but one way of breaking the evil spell caused by continual association with the inferior mind or minds, which spell will surely prove fatal if continued in, and is indeed proving fatal to thousands at the present day. That method is an entire separation from such mind or minds.

Such sundering of these injurious mental ties cannot, however, in every case be abrupt, or evils may result as great as those which it is sought to avoid. If a graft, however injurious, be roughly torn from the tree, the tree also is injured and perhaps destroyed. If your life has been one of long association with a lower mind, if both of you have, as previously stated, grown into a common life, and you are suddenly torn apart, the shock may prove to you injurious.

If one subsists for a long time on an injurious food, still a certain kind of life is derived from that food, and as the system has become accustomed to it, it cannot be immediately replaced by a healthier food. The system at first may not be able thoroughly to assimilate and digest such healthier food. There is a similar action and result as regards our mental diet.

Once be convinced of the evil resulting to you from any close, inferior association, and you will first assume in mind that such tie must be sundered. Assume this persistently. and half the work is done. That changed state of mind is the force then always working to free you, as your former state of mind, which endured, suffered, and submitted internally, was the force which bound you more and more firmly. The separation is now in your changed mental attitude simply a work of time. You have little to do, save to walt and take advantage of opportunities as they offer themselves. You have, in fact, committed yourself to another current of thought, and the forces coming of your changed mental condition and interior resolve are the spiritual correspondence of a great river to whose current you have committed yourself, and it is slowly bearing you away from your former enslaved condition. This is not a figurative illustration; change permanently a state of mind in which you have been for years; change unwilling submission into a hidden resolve no longer to submit; change endurance of near associations into a permanent and hidden resolve that you will separate from such associations; change that enforced content called "resignation to circumstances," as, for instance, resignation to the presence of inferior, squalid, and unpleasant material surroundings, into that positive internal mental attitude, which in plain language says--"I won't put up with this any longer; my body may be obliged to submit, endure, and suffer from these things temporarily, as it has done in the past, but in mind I will neither endure nor be resigned as I have been "–and you have placed yourself in the action of another power which will gradually bear you away from the old source of ill.

It is not so much what we *do* as what we *think* that brings results. By the force put out of what you permanently think are you carried, as on a current, to those results. You need do very little until you see that the time and opportunity has come for doing. It would be poor judgment for a man floating on a log down the Mississippi to keep on splashing the water and thereby using up his strength for the sake of "doing something." He had better remain quiet and take the chances of being picked up by a passing boat or steamer, or wait until he sees an opportunity of catching on to some near projecting headland. Then such strength as he may have been able to reserve will be used to some purpose. When you are in the right current of thought, you need in similar manner to reserve your strength until you meet the opportunity which that current will bring you, for as many injured through unwise and overmuch doing as by too little. If you don't know what to do, wait. When you wait till your hurry is over, you may see what really needs to be done.

Above all things, in any emergency or experience such as is suggested here, demand daily and hourly in silent thought the aid of a Higher Wisdom and Divine Power. There must come response to such demand. I do not assume to lay down a certain unbending rule to govern every individual life. Every individual life, when it places itself in the line of communication with its Higher Wisdom through a persistent mental attitude, asking silently for such wisdom, will make its own methods for riddance of the ills from which it desires to free itself, and such methods belong to it individually, nor can they safely be copied and used by anyone else. The Spirit of Infinite Good does not reveal itself alike to any two persons. The besetting error of our time is to copy or imitate other people's methods in everything, or to become blindly obedient to a book or the mind that wrote a book. Your mind, ever asking for Wisdom and Truth, is a power beyond any book and is now, or is to be, the reservoir into which ideas will flow which are different from those contained in any book. The power which generates and suggests new ideas is ever coming to the world. The book does not advance after it is written. But the mind which put ideas in that book may be ever going ahead and finding new meanings and broader interpretations for what it wrote years before.

If you wish to find out regarding the latest developments in chemistry or any material science, you do not have recourse to the books written a hundred years ago about such matters. You get the latest work on these subjects, and if possible you will go farther and get access to those now making such sciences their special studies, seeing that they may know something regarding them never yet written.

So even now in your own kingdom of mind there may be ideas and truths beyond any ever written, which you reject as "mere imaginings," or dare not assert either by word or act for fear of ridicule or opposition.

A book, like Paul, may plant new ideas in your mind; an individual like Apollos "may water" such ideas, but the awakened God in yourself can alone give the increase.

Complete isolation from their kind and loneliness is one terrible fear besetting some who live in associations which are really not congenial to them, but from which they dare not separate for fear of that loneliness. Try not to fear this. Permanent solitude is not in the order of Nature for anyone. Minds alike in thought were made to mingle and give each other pleasure. It is often the clinging to that order of association which, after all, only wearies you, and may oblige you often to play an enforced part to meet such association, that forms the barrier keeping you from your real companions. So long as (in mind) you accept the lower association, so long are you keeping the better away and sending it farther from you. So soon as you reject the lower (in mind), so soon do you set in motion the force to bring the better to you.

Chapter 7
REGENERATION; OR, BEING BORN AGAIN

WE do not yet know the full meaning or value of life.

The commonly held idea of existence runs thus: to be born, to grow from infancy to youth, from youth to maturity, from maturity to old age, from old age to death. During these stages, to gain possibly fame or fortune, but ever at the end to weaken, sicken, and die.

Man's real and ever-growing life is a condition so unlike this present existence, that there is scarcely a possibility of any realisation thereof by comparison between the two. If you had never seen anything of a tree but its roots in the dark, damp ground, could anyone by means of words convey to you a realisation of the beauty of its foliage and blossoms in the sunlight?

Our physical existence is the root from which in the future is to come an indescribable beauty and power.

Some speak lightly of their bodies, call them encumbrances, and entertain glowing anticipations, when rid of them, of a blissful life, entirely in the spiritual realm of existence.

This involves an error.

Because a certain physical life with ever-refining physical senses is in every stage of existence a necessity to the fullest complement of our lives.

The Christ of Judea spoke of the necessity of "Regeneration." "Ye must be born again," he Says.

Reincarnated we all have been many times. Regeneration is a step beyond reincarnation. Reincarnation means the total loss of one physical body and the getting of a new one through the aid of another organisation. Regeneration means the perpetuation of an ever refining physical body without that total separation of spirit and body called death.

The cruder the spirit, the longer were the intervals of time between its getting for itself a new physical body through reincarnation.

As the spirit was quickened and gained power, these intervals became less in duration, numbering years in place of centuries. With still greater increase of power the spirit will seek the regenerative instead of the reincarnative process of perpetuating its life of the physical senses.

A spiritualising and refining power has ever been and ever will be working on this planet. It has through innumerable ages changed all forms of being, whether mineral, animal, or vegetable, from coarse to finer types. It works with man as with all other organisations. It is ever changing him gradually from a material to a more spiritual being. It is carrying him through his many physical existences from one degree of perfection to another. It has in store for him new powers, new lives, and new methods of existence. That spiritual power has given him in the past new inventions. It illuminated his mind to see the uses of steam, electricity, and other material agencies. But far greater illumination is to come. A time is coming when he will not need iron, steam, and electricity to promote his convenience or enjoyment. New powers born out of his spiritual life will supersede the necessity of many of his present material aids.

There will come in the future a more perfected life, when, for the few at first and the many afterwards, there will be no physical death. In other words, every spirit will be able to use both its spiritual and physical senses, through the continual regeneration of its physical body.

Such making over and over again of the physical body will come of successive changes of mind. There will be continual separations from one old state of mind after another and entrances into new. We shall ever through regeneration be born into new individualities.

Regeneration may supersede reincarnation, because of our coming into a higher order of life, or receiving and being built of a higher order of thoughts. The spirit will then be ever changing its physical body for one still finer and more spiritualised. This is the process referred to by Christ as being "born again."

Life is an eternal series of regenerations. The whole aim and scope of all these writings is the endeavour to show what life really means; how the spiritual life rules the physical life; and how we are all growing from cruder to finer forms of life.

The spirit is regenerated when it shakes off the old physical body. It shakes off an old body because it is tired of carrying an instrument through which it cannot express itself. The old man or woman of decaying powers has as much mind or spirit as ever. But that mind cannot act on its body. It is cut off in a sense from that body. It is receding from that body and will finally quit it altogether. It recedes because, through ignorance, it has been drawing for years inferior thought and a monotonous round of thought to the body and endeavouring to make it over again with an old rotten material. It is like trying to repair a leaky roof with rotten shingles. This is the degenerative process of today and the cause of the decaying physical powers and death of the body.

But the more enlightened spirit will find out how to act on and replenish the body with newer and newer thought. This makes the body ever newer and newer and so keeps up the necessary connection between spirit and body.

We do not part with life in the loss of the physical body. But we do lose thereby one kind of life and a most important agency for the fullest enjoyment of life.

We lose in what is called death the use of that set of senses which we call the physical. We lose the power of living in a close connection with the world of physical things. It is most desirable to maintain a connection with the physical world, and the spirit on losing its body, contrary to general belief, laments the loss of such body and desires eagerly to have the possession and use of its former physical senses. Failing in this it uses, so far as it can. by a psychological law, the physical senses of those having bodies, whom it can influence or control.

Every living man and woman has such influence brought to bear on him or her from the unseen side of life.

The "dead," as they are falsely called, resume imperfectly their lives on earth, through aid unconsciously given them by the living, or, more properly speaking, by those living with physical bodies.

If we do not wish to find out the new--if we instantly reject what some may call "new-fangled ideas"–if we want to go on in the old way of our fathers, then we invite the company and mind of spirits as ignorant as ourselves, who will only help on the decay of our bodies after getting from them all the use they can.

These are "unregenerated spirits." They have drawn to them little new thought since losing their
bodies. They will by reason of the same ignorance through which they lost the last physical body, be drawn into another reincarnation, and perhaps another and another, until at last, gaining with each life more knowledge, they will know how to regenerate their bodies.

This regeneration will not come of any material medicines or methods. It will come of changing spiritual conditions. These spiritual conditions will cause the adoption of new habits and ways of life. But to adopt these habits before the spiritual condition prompts or demands them will do little good.

We have a life of the physical senses. We have another of the finer or spiritual senses. We live during the waking hours by the physical senses. We live another life during sleep by the spiritual senses. When these two lives are properly adjusted, they feed each other healthfully.

With such proper adjustment the physical senses receive a certain necessary supply of element from the spiritual while the body sleeps.

The spiritual being receives also from the material condition a certain vital supply. If your spirit loses its body these sources of mutual supply between body and spirit are for a time cut off.

The more perfected or regenerated life of the future means the consciousness of existence by both the physical and spiritual senses.

The life of the physical senses and that of the spiritual senses are necessary to each other. When they are joined together, and we become conscious of the use of both, life is relatively perfected and the spirit attains a degree of happiness not now to be imagined.

During all the centuries which have passed since Christ's time, can we point to any instance of this new birth or regeneration? If such regeneration is owing to a higher Faith and higher

Law, can we say that any persons, no matter what may have been their reputation for piety or uprightness, whose bodies have finally sickened and decayed, have lived up to the highest Law?

"The wages of sin is death," says the Bible. We would prefer to say that the result of an unperfected life is the death of the physical body.

The body of every weak, shrivelled, trembling old man or woman today is the result of sins committed in ignorance. Those sins lay in their thoughts. Out of such thought as it attracts the spirit builds first its spiritual body. The physical body is a material correspondence of the spiritual body. If the spirit believes in error it builds that error into the body. The result is decay.

For this result no blame can be imputed to those who suffer. They have lived up to all the light and knowledge they had. With more growth there will, in some condition of existence, come to them more knowledge. They will then see new methods of living and avoid the mistakes of the former less perfected life.

Charity comes of the knowledge that all people live up to the best light which they have. God alone can light up the darkened chambers of our and their minds. When we, leaving the faults of others alone, ask that our minds may be illuminated so as to see and avoid evil, that illumination alone will help all about us.

People weary of existence, because they think year after year the same set of thoughts and ideas over and over again. Eternal life and happiness come of a perpetual flow to us of new thought and idea. Thought is food for our spiritual beings. Our physical bodies are not nourished on one monotonous kind of food from year to year. Feed the spirit with the same thought (or try to) from year to year and it becomes sick. The sick spirit makes the sick body.

The Law of Eternal Life will not allow this repetition to go on. The Law says to us: "You were not made to run in ruts and grooves of fixed habit. You are not as John Smith or John Brown to be an eternal individuality without change, like a post rooted in the ground. You are to have a new mind for this period, and a superior mind with increased Powers of perception for the next period. You are ever, by drawing to you and adding to you new thought, to be as so many different individuals; as you live on, and this process of regeneration proceeds, you are born or changed into successive types of being, each one being finer than the last."

The regenerated life with a physical body means an ever-increasing life. It means a fresher capacity, with each day's waking, to sense that beauty in Nature which exists all around us. It means a new glory in each day's sunshine. It means a repose and restfulness whereby we can sit still and feel the spirit which animates the tree, the leaf, the ocean, the rivulet, the star, the flower, and every natural expression of the Infinite Mind. It means the daily flow to us of new thoughts which shall fill us with new life. It means that we shall rejoice in the realisation and firmly grounded faith that we have in us the possibilities for development into numberless new lives. It means that power of so losing our material self in any effort which we may make that all sense of time shall vanish and ennui and mental weariness shall be destroyed. It means power to live without drudgery of mind and body, or that anxiety which is even worse than drudgery. It means at last the getting of enjoyment from all things. To get enjoyment from everything Is to get life from everything. To get life from everything is to get power from all things. To get power implies a control of all physical elements. This includes a power of ever holding an ever-refining physical body.

Ennui is sickness. When we don't know what to do with ourselves, when we try to kill time and everything seems " flat, stale and unprofitable, we have temporarily lost our hold of the Great Fountain of life, the Supreme Mind and Power. We are absorbing the wearied thoughts of thousands around us, who think the same thing from day to day and from year to year, whose minds in their play are treadmills, who are trying to get Life, exhilaration and variety entirely out of physical things.

The true and regenerative life cannot be obtained from material things. That is the reason why all that money can buy fails to satisfy. The monster of discontent and ennui rages as much in the palace as the hovel. Solomon was in the claws of this beast when he said: "Vanity of vanities, all is vanity." That exclamation is a libel on the Infinite Mind. It came from the Jewish king, because he was trying to get life and happiness out of wood and stone and metal, and flesh and blood and all things material. It cannot be done.

But when, through demand of the Supreme, you get new thoughts, the material thing of yesterday seems to you as a new thing of today. The very rock which you passed yesterday has a new idea associated with it today. It may not be an idea which you can put in words. It is something which you feel rather than think. Myriads of thoughts, coming at the physical sight of all material things about us, are so felt, but can neither be talked out nor written out.

The regeneration of the body comes in response to our increasing demand of the Supreme Power to be led in the path of the Highest Wisdom. It comes of a courage gained at last of persistent demand, whereby we shall *dare* to trust entirely to that power. This it is doubtful if any can do at present. We try to trust in God, but when the pinch comes and things look dark, we are tempted to adopt some of our worn-out material methods for averting the evil. But perfect trust in the Supreme Power can gradually come to us. When it does men will become more than mortal. Whoever attains to such perfect trust will be regenerated.

Demand then new thoughts, and an increasing nearness to the Supreme Mind, and in time you receive new life, and all things about you are, for you, imbued with new life or idea. You are then in the line of the regenerative process. Your spirit, as well as your body, is being born again and again. It is drawing to it ever new ideas, and becomes literally a new spirit, a new being. If the spirit is being thus renewed or regenerated, the body must be also.

As we become more spiritualised, as the material mind gives place more and more to the Spiritual Mind; in other words, as the regenerative process goes on, we shall, from time to time, find ourselves prompted to change many of our habits and modes of life. These changes will involve eating, sleeping, and association.

But we need not try to force these changes on ourselves. The regenerative process will involve the eating of less and less animal food, until we shall eat none whatever. But there would be nothing gained from ceasing to eat meat before the desire for It had gone.

The regenerative process will impel us at times to seek solitude, because when alone with Nature the spirit absorbs and assimilates a finer quality of thought. But to enforce on ourselves the solitude of the hermitage or cloister when there is no real love for it does little good, as is proved by the fact that hermit and recluse have physically decayed and died like the rest.

This regeneration of the body will come to no one directly from any system of forms, habits, or observances. It will come because of a time ripe for it to come. As this planet ripens spiritually all material things upon it partake of that ripening or development. The life of today, so different and superior to that of five hundred or a thousand years ago, is a part and a proof of that development. The earth ripened first from chaos to coarse development in the animal and vegetable kingdoms of ages ago, and then to its present relatively more refined condition. But this refining process is never to cease.

Perhaps you will say on reading this, "What has all this to do with me? What you say may be true. But it is all too far off, too indefinite. I want something to benefit me now."

This idea of the body's regeneration is for you a benefit now, if you can accept it. It cannot be displaced from your mind. It will first, as a tiny seed, stay there. It may for months or years show no sign of life and seem to be forgotten. But it will grow and have more and more of a place in your thought. It will gradually change the quality of your thoughts. It will gradually force out an old and false interpretation of life and bring in a new one. It will impel you to look ever forward to newer joys and make you cease groping among regrets and sad remembrances of your past, when you know that such thoughts bring decay and death to the body. We are built literally of our thoughts. When we realise that our regrets, our envyings and jealousies, our borrowings of trouble, or our morbid contemplations of subjects ghastly and sickly, are literally things, and bad things, actually put in our bodies, as such thoughts, materialising themselves from invisible to visible element, turn into flesh and blood, and that as so built into ourselves they bring us pains, aches, weakness, sickness, wrinkles, bowed backs, weak knees and failing powers, we have a good and tangible reason for getting rid of them.

The body of a person given over to melancholy will be literally built of gloomy thoughts materialised into flesh and blood.

When a girl realises more and more clearly that jealousy, peevishness, and pettish pouting moods will spoil her good looks and complexion, she will make efforts to rid herself of such thoughts. They will destroy her body. The Infinite Power for good wants all things and all people to be beautiful, healthful and symmetrical, and intends ever to increase this beauty, health, and symmetry. It works through a continual process ot regeneration to keep them so. If it cannot effect such perpetual life and beauty with one physical organisation, it mercifully lets it go to pieces and gives the spirit another.

When a man realises that his angry mood, or his covetous mood, or his grumbling mood represents so much material put in his body, and that such element will give his body pain and make it sick, he has a good strong reason for having some care as to what his mind runs on, and for making the "inside of the platter clean."

Let us remember, so far as we can, that every unpleasant thought is a bad thing literally put in the body. Are some people unpleasant to us? Do their airs or affectations, or their stinginess or dishonesty, or their domineering manners, or their coarseness and vulgarity, offend us? Well, let us try and forget them. Why talk them over for an hour, holding the while all their disagreeable traits in our minds, and think of them, maybe, for hours afterwards, when we know that these unpleasant images which we carry in mind are *things* which are being literally put in our bodies to affect them injuriously and degenerate them? All such thoughts we must get rid of.

Such riddance is the commencement of getting a new body. It is in the way of a literal regeneration. If through long habit we find that we cannot by our own endeavour keep out of these injurious moods, if we find ourselves from time to time drawn into the current of tattle, or greed, or envy, we can cease all endeavour of our own and ask help of the Supreme Power to give us new and better thoughts. That Power, through our demand, will give us a new mind. The new mind will bring the new body.

Made in United States
North Haven, CT
01 April 2025

67479979R00033